The Years of Silence Are Past

The Years of Silence Are Past

My Father's Life with Bipolar Disorder

STEPHEN P. HINSHAW

University of California, Berkeley

CAMBRIDGE
UNIVERSITY PRESS

PUBLISHED BY THE PRESS SYNDICATE OF THE UNIVERSITY OF CAMBRIDGE
The Pitt Building, Trumpington Street, Cambridge, United Kingdom

CAMBRIDGE UNIVERSITY PRESS
The Edinburgh Building, Cambridge CB2 2RU, UK
40 West 20th Street, New York, NY 10011-4211, USA
477 Williamstown Road, Port Melbourne, VIC 3207, Australia
Ruiz de Alarcón 13, 28014 Madrid, Spain
Dock House, The Waterfront, Cape Town 8001, South Africa

http://www.cambridge.org

First published 2002

Printed in the United States of America

Typefaces New Aster 11/15 pt. and ITC Symbol   *System* LaTeX 2_ε [TB]

A catalog record for this book is available from the British Library.

Library of Congress Cataloging in Publication Data

Hinshaw, Stephen P.
  The years of silence are past: my father's life with bi-polar disorder / Stephen
P. Hinshaw.
    p.   cm.
  Includes bibliographical references and index.
  ISBN 0-521-81780-3
  1. Hinshaw, Virgil, 1919–1995. 2. Manic-depressive illness – Patients – United
States – Biography.   3. Depressed persons – United States – Biography.   4. Manic-
depressive illness.   5. Hinshaw, Stephen P. I. Title

RC516.H54 H54 2003
616.89′5′20092 – dc21
[B]   2002019186

ISBN 0 521 81780 3 hardback

To the memory of my father, Virgil G. Hinshaw, Jr.,
and to my mother and my sister

Contents

Foreword

We all sail with sealed orders, as Herman Melville put it. We do not know where we will end up or how we will get there. We have only our own experience and that of others to give us any inkling. Children look to their parents for the early maps and for reassurance that they will somehow find their way. For most of us, this is enough – although nothing is ever really enough – to give us a fair start on our life's sailings. But what happens if a parent has himself lost his way?

Stephen Hinshaw, who is a professor of psychology at the University of California, Berkeley, has written a powerful account of what it is to be the son of a man who lost not only his way, but his mind as well. Hinshaw's father, a highly regarded professor of philosophy, suffered from increasingly severe attacks of manic-depressive, or bipolar, illness, for which he was repeatedly institutionalized. Hinshaw portrays his father's struggles with clear-eyed compassion and describes vividly the complexity of their relationship: his beholdenness to his father for much of what he most values in himself, his intellect and curiosity, and his sharp fear that his own intense moods might someday veer out of control as his father's had. Woven around his personal story is the story of an illness – a painful and genetic mental illness – and its often frightening effects on those who live in its wake.

Professor Hinshaw has written a compelling book about fathers and sons, madness, and the intolerance of society and the academic and medical communities. Dr. Hinshaw was one of my first clinical psychology interns when I was a young assistant professor at the UCLA Neuropsychiatric Institute. It was clear to those of us on the faculty that he would go far in his intellectual pursuits. He has. He has also written an excellent book, one that will go far beyond the academic world, and for that I am particularly delighted.

Kay Redfield Jamison, Ph.D.
Professor of Psychiatry
The Johns Hopkins School of Medicine

Acknowledgments

A number of people have encouraged me in my efforts to tell this story. For such support and for comments on earlier drafts, my heartfelt thanks go to Stuart Ablon, Cari Anderson, Diana Baumrind, William Beardslee, Richard Beery, Caryn Carlson, Nancy Chodorow, John Coie, Carolyn Cowan, Phil Cowan, Joan Davidson, Daphne de Marneffe, Glen Elliott, Margaret Farruggio, Barbara Geller, Leslie Gunsalus, Forrest Hamer, Enrico Jones, Kim Josephs, Peter Jensen, Charles King, Rachel Klein, Ann Kring, William Lamb, Steve Lee, Bob Levenson, Steve Lopez, Laura Mason, Jennie McDonald, Clark McKown, Jeff Measelle, Amy Mezulis, Kate Moses, Liz Owens, Mac Runyan, Amy Schaffer, Cassandra Simmel, Jennifer Treuting, Linda Mans Wagener, Rhona Weinstein, John Weisz, Christine Zalecki, and Brian Zupan.

I wish to pay special tribute to those individuals who have given extraordinary encouragement. John Richters, whose disclosures of his own past for the media are a study in openness, urged me to write up the details of our conversations about my father that we began to have a number of years ago. With his always unerring sense of wordcraft, he also emphasized to me the double meaning of the word "bipolarities" featured in this work. Kay Redfield Jamison was an inspiration to me as both a clinical teacher and supervisor and, more recently, a model of personal disclosure. I thank her for challenging me to take the steps I have taken. Gaye Carlson provided important support for earlier versions of this work, giving me a sense of the history behind her pathbreaking research on the stages of mania, which included the realization that psychosis was often part of the manic spectrum. Her commitment to responsive clinical care and sound research is precisely what the field needs. Suzanne Gassner is the gifted psychologist noted in the text who suggested the alternative title for this work ("Just Don't Talk About It"), based on her keen clinical insights and her own family experiences. Mark Elin, the other gifted clinician cited herein, helped me to understand both the lasting impact of psychosis in a family and the lasting impact of friendship – ours. Sir Michael Rutter graciously commented on an early draft, reinforcing the story's importance and presciently predicting that there would be significant professional resistance to uncovering some of American psychology and psychiatry's historic past. Rob Kelly has been a thoughtful and steady source of encouragement to be open in my writing and in my life. Rob, thanks for the support, and welcome to fatherhood. David Donovan generously and perceptively commented on earlier drafts and made my father feel welcome at the last academic conference he ever attended. Lisa Capps, whose loss is felt daily by everyone whose life she touched, provided instantaneous feedback on this work whenever I needed comments. Through her effervescence and wisdom, she encouraged me when, on occasion, I felt like giving up. Dacher Keltner has been his usual enthusiastic self in his encouragement, making incisive comments and pushing me to clarify key passages. Dante Cicchetti has epitomized support and enthusiasm. Indeed, our joint work on stigma and mental disorder freed me to take the present writing to new levels. Julia Hough, my editor at Cambridge University Press, has been nothing but encouraging. Her grasp of the essential message of these words was a genuine pleasure to behold, and her skills as an editor are considerable.

Finally, Kelly Campbell Hinshaw, my wife, has been patient, giving, and wise in her support and love, urging me always to consider the "big picture" and to increase my understanding of and empathy for my mother's experience throughout this life story. I write these words full of hope for our future together, along with my stepson John Neukomm and my son Jeffrey Wyn Hinshaw.

The Years of Silence Are Past

My grandfather, Virgil Hinshaw, Sr., and my grandmother, Eva Piltz Hinshaw (early 1920s).

My father, Virgil Hinshaw, Jr., at the age of one, late 1920.

"The Motherless Hinshaw Boys," Randall, Robert, Virgil Jr., and Harold, 1923. This photograph appeared in *World Dry*, an international temperance/prohibition publication, vol. 2, no. 4.

My father, at the time of his graduation from Pasadena Junior College, at the age of nineteen (summer 1939). From an inscription on the back, addressed to his great uncle: "Happy New Year from your great-nephew, Virgil Hinshaw Jr., who this year, 1939, was sent to Minnesota to contest for oratorical honors among Junior College students. Stood 6th highest nationally." He entered Stanford University in the fall.

The six Hinshaw brothers in Pasadena, California, in 1950 (left to right): Harold (age 37), Randall (34), Robert (32), Virgil Jr. (30), Harvey (24), and Paul (22).

My father and me, in the backyard of our first home (1953).

My first-grade picture, age five (fall 1958), which my father always kept in his wallet. He said I showed a "Mona Lisa" smile in this picture.

My father and me, vacationing in Florida (spring 1959).

My sister, Sally, and me, vacationing in Niagara Falls (summer 1959).

Perfecting a hook shot, age twelve (1965).

My father and me, in our backyard in Columbus, Ohio, around 1973. He is fifty-three and I am twenty. By that time, it was two years that we had been having our talks in his study during my vacations from college.

My father and me, in Southern California, about 1983, when I had finished graduate school. He is in his early sixties, and I am around thirty. By this time, our talks were focusing on his diagnosis of bipolar disorder and his treatment with lithium.

Seven years later, the early stages of Parkinson's disease have aged my father considerably.

At my father's gravesite, Columbus, Ohio, five months after his death (December 1995).

My son, Jeffrey, and me, at my father's gravesite (summer 1997).

Introduction

Images of my father:

(1) Athletic, intelligent boy in a religious, high-achieving family of six brothers, coping with the loss of his mother at age three and with the Great Depression during his late childhood and early adolescence, through academic and athletic attainment and his devout religious faith... versus a sixteen-year-old adolescent, jumping from the porch roof in a delusional attempt to stop fascism, then housed in a county psychiatric hospital ward for half a year, tied to his bed, nearly starving himself for fear of being poisoned.

(2) Acclaimed young scholar, educated at Stanford and Princeton, interacting with the leading minds of the century, in an ascendant career as a philosopher... versus a frightened man in his thirties, staring out the front window at home following psychiatric hospitalizations and electroshock treatments, asking his wife to help him remember the names of his neighbors.

(3) Husband and father, professor, singer in the church choir, gentle discloser of his life story to his son... versus a frail, anxious, sometimes bewildered septuagenarian, rigid with Parkinson-like illness yet still grateful for the richness of his life.

Such contrasts are clearly bipolar, signifying the presence of opposites, of extremes. Even now, I wonder about how they could

1

have occurred in the same person. "Bipolar" rating scales are those that include opposing poles of the quality being described, for example, "Rate this family from overly involved *to* overly distant*" or "this film from* unwatchable *to* one of the year's best.*" My father's history epitomizes a wide bipolarity of functioning throughout his life.*

Indeed, the mental disorder from which he suffered is known as bipolar disorder. *Formerly called manic-depressive illness, this condition is marked by recurrent episodes of extreme moods, ranging from flat, empty depressions to elated, expansive, and ultimately chaotic manias. In other words, from despair to madness, often with recovery to normal functioning in between. As his story indicates, however, the bipolar contrasts in afflicted individuals far transcend mood states, permeating nearly every aspect of their lives.*

Coming to terms with such bipolarities is a source of major struggle for the person suffering from such major mental disorder. How does one maintain a sense of self, or any semblance of stability, while weathering these switches, which can involve grandiose self-absorption, utter lack of judgment, regrettable acts, and suicidal thoughts and behaviors?

Related bipolarities also reverberate through the lives of those close to the person with manic-depressive illness. Family members must cope with not only the sufferer's swings of mood but also the guilt, shame, and even terror that the episodes create for their own lives. Friends may understandably wonder what on earth is happening, given the extremes of emotion and behavior they are witnessing. Workmates, fellow students, and other personal contacts may feel perplexed, mystified, and even enraged at the sudden shifts in mood and behavior.

As my father's son, I have experienced a number of bipolarities throughout my life. Some of these seem ingrained in my personality, reflecting a certain temperament: an energy and drive, along with a particular tendency toward sadness – traces, perhaps,

*of my father's genetic legacy. Yet other bipolarities appear to ema-
nate more from the years of silence about my father's condition
that I experienced as a child, coupled with my gradual learning
about his life as I matured. They play themselves out in questions
that I have long asked: Should I express my fears or stay in
control? Are my own accomplishments adequate, or can I really
ever measure up to my father's potential? Is the family tree blessed
or cursed?*

*Coming to terms with such bipolarities is a key reason for
writing this book.*

It is a landmark time for the entire field of mental health.
Research funding is increasing. Scientific understanding
of fundamental brain processes is advancing at a staggering
rate.[1] Real advances in the treatment of serious mental disorder are emerging. And most important of all, societal views
and conceptions of mental illness may finally be changing.
With gathering force, mental disorders are "coming out of the
closet" in terms of public recognition, open discussion, policy
change, and personal disclosure.[2] Both in the United States
and internationally, momentum is building.

First, the highest levels of government in the United States
have officially recognized the impact of mental disorder. In
June 1999, President Bill Clinton and Tipper Gore sponsored
the first-ever White House Conference on Mental Health. In
December of that same year, the Surgeon General, David
Satcher, M.D., released the first report on mental disorders
ever to emanate from that office.[3] Both the White House Conference and the Surgeon General's Report gave testimony to
the huge numbers of individuals and families afflicted with
mental disorder, the lack of adequate diagnosis and treatment for a distressingly large proportion of such persons,
the need for continued advances in research on causes and

interventions, the shame and stigmatization that too often attend mental illness even today, and the types of policy change that are necessary to remedy current inadequacies and inequities. Indeed, mental disorders are now recognized to rival the major physical diseases (cancer, heart disease, infectious diseases) as the leading causes of economic, physical, and psychological burden worldwide.[4]

Second, media awareness is surging. For instance, in this country the National Mental Health Awareness Campaign has produced poignant, youth-oriented media "spots" about eating disorders, depression, and suicide, which have aired on MTV and major networks.[5] As an example of international efforts, the Royal College of Psychiatrists in the United Kingdom has initiated a five-year campaign to reduce the stigma and prejudice that surround mental disorder, through a program entitled "Changing Minds: Every Family in the Land." Included in this effort are eye-catching websites and brochures, with realistic and pointed information on the effects of mental disorder.[6] In addition, television and cinema are depicting mental disorder with greater reality and unprecedented sympathy: Witness *A Beautiful Mind* with Russell Crowe, which appeared as a major motion picture late in 2001 and which recently garnered the Academy Award for best picture.

Third, changes in policy are appearing. Federal laws in the United States have begun to insist on "parity," whereby mental disorders receive the same access to care and funding for treatment as do physical illnesses. Enforcement of recent statutes is not yet consistent, and more potent legislation regarding parity has recently been rejected by the U.S. Congress,[7] but a start has been made.

Fourth, publication of personal and family accounts of mental disorder is increasing rapidly. A sizable bibliography now exists.[8] Most of these accounts are biographical or autobiographical narratives, but books and articles about the experiences of family members are also emerging.[9] In addition, Wahl's large-scale national questionnaire survey, which included detailed interviews of a selected subgroup of the participants, has yielded both quantitative and qualitative information about the enormous problems that mentally disordered individuals still face in terms of discrimination, scapegoating, and stigma.[10] Overall, although gaining a job or obtaining health insurance may be threatened when one discloses a history of mental illness, it is no longer as rare, daring, or unacceptable as it used to be to disclose personal or familial experiences with serious mental disorder.

Real questions therefore emerge: Is there any room for another family account? What more might be gained from an additional story? After asking myself these questions repeatedly, I have concluded that my father's story is indeed worth telling. For one thing, the progress noted above in terms of political recognition, media awareness, and policy change is still incomplete. For example, stereotypes still abound, and parity is not yet a reality. Even more, my reasons are intensely personal. Hearing my father recount his story to me profoundly changed and deepened my own life, undoubtedly influencing my choice of career as a clinical psychologist and professor. My understanding of his story has also brought me closer to answering lingering questions that I have asked myself for many years: Why did my father disappear, from time to time, without explanation? Was he sane? How did he come back from the devastation he experienced? Why do so many relatives seem to have mental illnesses as well? How did my family cope when I was a child – and might there be more open and disclosing ways of doing so? Why, in fact, do so few people ever seem to want to talk about mental illness, beyond jokes, cruelty, or redirection of the topic? And most fundamentally, how much must I fear losing control myself – control over my mental functions, my life, my stability? Given the strong personal and professional investment I have in such questions, I attempt to provide at least some answers in this book.

I also believe that my father's story contains important, even universal messages about the experience and consequences of mental disorder. As personal as the story is to me and my family, the clear and depressing fact is that millions of individuals and families experience the isolation, confusion, hopelessness, and destructiveness of serious mental illness. The more that such issues are talked about openly, the better, because the cloak of secrecy and shame that still surrounds these problems may come to be replaced by openness and compassion. For that reason alone, the story is worth telling.

Also, despite the grim realities of many aspects of my father's personal history, including the shortcomings of the mental health profession in recognizing and dealing with his condition, I believe that his story is ultimately a positive one. From my perspective, his life illustrates the essential point that devastating and even debilitating life experiences can yield strength, gentleness, and resilience. Too often, mental illness is portrayed as both entirely irrational and completely dominating of the afflicted person's life. This perspective, however, neglects the reality that mental illness is a major part of the human condition, showing its effects in nearly every extended family on the planet, and that it can prompt courage and strength as well as devastation and hopelessness, often in unexpected ways.

In the latter portions of my narrative account, I discuss key clinical and scientific themes raised by my father's life story. These include the complex array of causal factors that generate serious mental disorder, the struggle for the individual to maintain a coherent self-concept throughout chaotic episodes of disturbance, and the interplay of inner and outer worlds

Introduction

(i.e., of psychological plus societal forces) in mental disturbance. I hope that these topics come to life in the context of my father's vivid life history.

At the outset, I must emphasize that that there is tremendous variation among individuals who suffer from bipolar disorder or from any other category of mental affliction. The uniqueness of my father's life means that there are many aspects of mental disorder that are not contained in these pages. Indeed, his episodes tended to feature the manic "pole" of bipolar disorder, with less clearly demarcated (though still real) depressive episodes. Life, however, does not imitate textbooks, and my father's story contains both unique and universal elements. My hope is that the issues I raise are of interest to persons who suffer from mental disorder, to their family members, to scientists and clinicians in the field – especially those in training – and to large segments of the general public.

Because my own perspectives are closely intertwined with my father's story, I also describe some of my own experiences and reactions as a son. That is, I convey several of the roles I played in his life: listener, confidant, and, in later years, caretaker-at-a distance. I also recount my own early memories of my father, my mystification for many years about his absences, some important milestones that I encountered as I matured and learned of his story, and the lasting impact that his disclosures and life story have had on me. I also describe some of the struggles I encountered as a young adult, related as they were to my growing understanding of his condition and history. Yet I aim to keep my father as the main focus, hoping that my personal perspectives can help to reveal him more clearly.

Most of the major material for this narrative emanates from discussions that my father and I had over a period of twenty-five years, beginning in my first year of college, when I began to return to the family home for holidays. I also incorporate excerpts from his handwritten notes and typed autobiographical material, most of which he wrote in the last two decades of his life. The narrative also incorporates verbal accounts from family members, chiefly my mother and several of my fathers' brothers and colleagues. I also utilize excerpts from letters written by my father, my paternal grandfather, and other relatives, letters that have been saved in family files for many years.

My mother's perspective is crucial to my father's story, but I have tried to respect her understandable desire for privacy. Living with a partner or spouse with serious mental disorder can be confounding, exhausting, and even terrifying, especially when secrecy, shame, and lack of professional assistance are the norm, as was the case throughout much of my parents' lives. My mother was the foundation of the family for decades, as the following words make clear. Although there is another set of stories and issues about the rest of my family that I could recount, this work is primarily my father's story.

My father's description of his life to me, beginning when I entered college and unfolding throughout the rest of his days, uncovered a reality that surpassed anything I had ever encountered. Perhaps my perspective is self-centered, but I can't help but think that others will be affected by its "bipolar" content, alternately disturbing and moving, harrowing and transcendent, mundane and profound. Because of such factors as family silence early in my life, the potential stigma and shame of divulging the content in these pages, the real desire for privacy on the part of family members, and my struggle in blending my father's voice with my own, it has not been an easy story for me to try to convey. On the whole, however, I have found it exciting to portray the life experiences of my father and to document the challenges that lie ahead for those who live with and work with mental disorder. I still hold a strong desire that many of the events described in these pages had not happened,

Introduction

but silence is part of the denial and distancing about mental illness that I hope to overcome. I write with the hope that my father's experiences may help to educate, to inspire reflection and action, and to foster deeper understanding of both the painful and the resilient aspects of the human condition that relate to mental disorder.

1

Beginnings

The time is the late 1950s. The house is suburban, colonial-style, the first story brick and the second white clapboard, symmetrical in design. Across the Olentangy River, not far away, is a large Midwestern University, Ohio State: the huge stadium, the land-grant buildings, the philosophy department housed in the flagship building on campus, a handsome brick labyrinth. It is a fall evening, cooling off rapidly, now that it is dark.

My father: mid-thirties, athletic build, round and expressive face, black hair peaked in front as it sweeps back from its part. Professor of philosophy, interested in theory of knowledge, logic, the progress of science in the twentieth century. Quick to an infectious smile, yet often introspective; lover of intellectual discussion about fundamental scientific and philosophical questions. He had moved to Columbus a decade before to teach at Ohio State, where his career as a philosopher has been in ascendancy. He often strikes an academic pose, thoughtfully smoking his pipe while reading or holding forth with academic discussions.

My mother: brown-eyed, solemn yet beautiful, still tan from the summer. She had grown up in Columbus, attended Ohio State for her bachelor's and master's degrees, met her future husband through the university, and settled into suburban life with him, a life closely tied to the university.

Beginnings

The couple has two young children: I am three and a half, and my sister is two and a half.

My mother has seen the signs before, over the past few years: A particular glint in her husband's eye, a too-ready smile, a penchant for nonstop talking, a different level of energy. A sure sign is his playing, at volumes far too loud, religious choral music on the phonograph. At these times it feels to her that a chemical change is overtaking him, although she gets nowhere when she tries to tell any doctors of this intuition. She knows what is bound to ensue with him: grand plans, sleeplessness, irritability, increasing irrationality, and paranoia, soon followed by utter disorganization. On some occasions, he has required hospitalization, and she is left with taking care of the household and the children, having to "cover" in front of friends and relatives. No one has really dwelled on it, but the term schizophrenia has floated in the air. When his episodes are over, however, they are really over, as mysteriously as they had begun. He acts as though nothing has happened, without discussion. Silence lingers between the couple.

Back to the fall evening: The hour is getting late, as it is now after 10 p.m. A popular variety show is on the television, broadcast from Cincinnati, 100 miles away from Columbus. An attractive female singer is singing this evening. My father has seen her on this program before, but tonight it is different: He has become obsessed with her. He believes, in fact, that her lyrics are communicating messages to him. He needs to see her, to continue the communication in person. It is urgent.

For a week or more, his behavior has been escalating, increasingly energetic, enthusiastic, bombastic. My mother's worry increases daily: Where will it stop this time?

Growing even more excited and agitated with the show, my father contends that they must drive to Cincinnati to find the singer, so that he can respond to her messages. The idea takes complete hold of him; he can't let it go.

11

My mother is terrified: to Cincinnati, in the car, at this time of night? She knows better than to try and talk him out of such a plan when he has reached this state, as his anger will escalate. So should she let him drive off – and perhaps learn of a fatal accident the next day, given his growing impatience and irrationality? Or should she accompany him to Cincinnati... but then what of the children? There is no reasoning with him; he must leave. Thinking fast, she decides to go along, fighting her terror that the children may awaken in the night with no one to look after them.

One last thought: Could she call anyone at this late hour? Even if she did, what would she say? And there's no opportunity to wait for someone to arrive, given her husband's impatience and force. What can she do? Maybe her presence will somehow contain him.

They head for the family car, a 1956 Ford Victoria with a strong engine, and tear off in a southwesterly direction. The inter-state highway system does not yet exist, and the roads are mostly two-lane highways. Yet he drives frightfully fast, possessed of his need. At speeds of over 90 miles per hour, they fly through the night. Does she dare allow herself too many thoughts of the children, asleep at home?

Somehow they arrive in Cincinnati after 11:30 p.m., managing to find the TV station from which the show had originated, its huge broadcasting tower providing a beacon. Almost as if in a dream – but if this is a dream, it's fast becoming a nightmare – my father insists on leaving the car to enter the station and find the singer. My mother fears for an ugly confrontation at the front desk. Fortunately, the hour is late enough that the gates are locked.

She struggles to maintain composure, concentrating on rein-ing him in. Will he try to jump the fence? She talks simply and rationally, convincing him that the singer has left and that there is no use in staying. His internal struggle is apparent, but finally he relents, suddenly eager to return home. They roar back onto the highway. She can't believe the speedometer. What if a highway patrolman were to pull them over, with her husband in his state? Will there be a physical confrontation? Will they end up in jail? What will happen when the children awaken?

Luck is with them, however, and they make it back to Columbus safely by the wee hours of the morning, racing over the rolling hills of Southern Ohio as they flatten out into the farmland plains of Central Ohio. She can't believe it; they are back in the driveway at home. Heart in her throat, she rushes upstairs to find the two children still asleep in their beds, oblivious to the disruption and absence. Her heart begins to slow, but the terror hasn't left. How long can this last? she wonders, relieved, terrified, wishing for some rest. What is next?

I know nothing of these events at the time. It wasn't until much later, in fact, that I began to learn of such parts of our family history. Could they really have happened? Did life really go on, as these episodes intensified? How could my parents have kept the details from my sister and me, for years to come? What is the impact of such events on a family, on young children ... or even on the adults that these young children become?

To begin to answer these questions, I take up my father's earliest years, far from Columbus, far from professorship, marriage, and the reception of messages across the television waves. In the process, I also describe those in my father's family, whose lives were marked by both high achievement and mental disturbance.

Virgil Goodman Hinshaw, Jr., was born in LaGrange, Illinois, outside of Chicago, on November, 3, 1919. He was the youngest of four boys. His father's namesake, he was called "Junior" by all family members. Family legend has it that, after delivering her fourth boy, my grandmother told her husband, "This one, you may call Virgil."

The home was middle-class. The family did not live in grand style, but comfortably. Their lives were devoted to education, work, and religion, with a clear flavor of social action from their Quaker and Methodist roots. There was a strong sense of purpose in the home, given my grandfather's central role in the Prohibition movement and my grandmother's missionary background.

From early accounts, Junior was an outgoing and engaging toddler. His father wrote to relatives, when Junior was just over two years of age:

> The boys are certainly a lively bunch. . . . Junior has to have me, each morning, go down and run him in a race in the basement and then return and be his tiger by getting down on all fours and having him on my back and I must say "ooo, ooo, ooo, ooo" and scare all the others at the same time.

Life in the home was active and fulfilling, with a growing family of boys and with national success related to Prohibition.

My father's first memory is of an event that occurred when he was three years old. Throughout his life, he remembered that, early in 1923, he was standing in the family living room, next to a large box (a coffin, though he didn't know the term at the time), in which lay the body of his mother. She had died suddenly, in her early forties, of a hemorrhage following surgery for an ovarian tumor. In a typed manuscript produced when he was in his sixties, filed with a host of personal papers and academic materials, my father put his memory into words:

> I vaguely remember her funeral in our home – all the older people milling about and then some men talking about her life. The next morning I remember being held up over the open casket (with my next-oldest brother) by my father and

being told: "This is your mother. She's asleep. You'll never see her again."*

During conversations that my father and I had about his life as I matured into adulthood, he often returned to this first memory, showing me pictures of his mother (who had ballooned in weight to well over 200 pounds in her last years) and commenting on the sternness and finality of his father's words regarding her death.

In a letter my grandfather wrote to a relative several months after his wife's death, he stated that Junior was inconsolable at nights, crying for his mother, while his three older brothers attempted to calm him and help him get to sleep. My grandfather was a national leader in the Prohibition movement. A major Prohibition newsletter, published later that year, prominently displayed a photograph of four young brothers, aged three to ten years, posing in and behind a wagon, under the poignant headline "The Motherless Hinshaw Boys."

My father's manuscript from his later life continues with the narrative of his early years:

> Not long after her death, my father decided to move his brood of four boys to the West where he had relatives. After a visit in Greenleaf, Idaho, on our uncle's apple farm where we met cousins galore, our father took us on to Tacoma, Washington. . . . Memories of this phase of my early life include taking the ferry boat from Tacoma to Seattle . . . and my somehow

---

* Regarding this quote, my father's older brother, Randall, nearly eight years old when their mother died, had a slightly different memory. When I was an adult, he told me that he had also been present at the time of his father's pronouncement, distinctly recalling an addition to the last sentence: "You'll never see her again *in this life.*" This last phrase gave him hope, he noted, in that he took from it the belief that he might someday see his mother in heaven. Junior was probably too young to have processed or remembered this qualification.

contracting double bronchial pneumonia. I surely remember the long period of recovery from that disease and how worried the family was about me. . . . I vividly remember lying on a bed with ice bags everywhere to reduce my temperature. Even more stimulating were the constant and very cold enemas I received. . . .

The family without a mother acquired one when they moved to Lankershim (now North Hollywood), California. In late 1924 my father remarried . . . she had been a missionary in South America and Mexico for a dozen years. She embraced me, literally and figuratively, as her own, and I came to love her very much. Yet, as I found out especially when we moved shortly to Pasadena, that embrace entailed a loss of the freedom I had been used to in the 18 months since my mother's passing. No doubt I had been living in a kind of dream world where I could do about what I wanted without [sic] impunity. As I was to learn, we never appreciate our liberty until it is taken away from us. . . . I became conscious of my loss of liberty through strict discipline in the presence of my stepmother – my "Mother" as she soon became.

With the family now settled in Pasadena, in a modest, California-style, two-story house on a street lined with palm trees, the older boys attended public schools while Junior played in the neighborhood and helped around the household. The next year, he began to attend kindergarten. In a letter sent by his stepmother to her sister, when Junior was five years of age, she comments on his mischievous side:

One day this week I was out in front, buying vegetables from the vegetable man, when I saw the children coming home from school down the street. I heard Junior's voice ring out roughly, "Shut up! Don't blow your nose so loud. I'll knock you in the bean!" I came in thinking that was pretty rough and strong coming from one five year old, so as soon as he came in, I asked him, "Junior, were you saying all those

things to the little boy down the street that you play with?"
He looked a little blank, and then shook his head and said,
"No, I didn't say it to *him*." Then I asked, "Who did you say
it to? They were pretty rough sounding words to anybody."
He then said, "I didn't say it to anybody." And then he began
to cry...and amid his sobs he said, "I said it to the *wind*."
Would that not get to you? The *wind*! Anyway, even to the
wind they were not nice words to be yelling on the street.

This seemingly delightful story, however, ends with an ominous footnote. On a copy of this letter kept in his files, my
father had added, many years later, a handwritten annotation
in the margin:

When I had finished crying, I was asked to go to the bathroom
and bare my buttocks in the corner for spanking. "Never say
shut up to anyone or anything," said my mother.

Indeed, the discipline he received from his stepmother, which
I discuss in the next chapter, remained vividly in his mind
throughout his life.

At this point, a brief sketch of the family history may be helpful. I begin with my grandfather. Virgil Goodman Hinshaw,
Sr., was born in 1876 on a farm in Iowa. The third of four children, he was one and a half years old when his father died.
His mother took over the family farm, which subsequently
suffered financial losses at the hands of her second husband,
my grandfather's stepfather. My grandfather and his siblings
worked from 4:00 a.m. each day, as children and adolescents,
to maintain the property, which eventually thrived. Quaker
meetings were the other major activity of the household.
Educated as a lawyer and a practicing Quaker throughout his
life, he had joined the "Band of Hope," the children's branch
of the Women's Christian Temperance Union at age twelve and
became centrally involved in the growing temperance movement early in his career. From all accounts, he was a serious

man (though one with a wry sense of humor), highly energetic, pragmatic, and dedicated to his cause.

His relatives include a number of successful professionals. Among his cousins was one of the first woman physicians in the West, and others were entrepreneurs. Another, Corwin Hinshaw, born in 1903 (and recently deceased at the age of ninety-seven), had a career as a renowned medical scientist, who was on a team discovering and performing early clinical trials on one of the first modern antibiotics used to treat tuberculosis. International awards accumulated throughout his career.

Other relatives, however, did not share such success. Several had spent many years in mental hospitals. Psychoses and even occasional suicides were present. Another cousin of my grandfather's died, in her late twenties, subsequent to what appeared to be years of living with an eating disorder. In the current parlance, the family history is "loaded" – loaded, that is, with mental disorder.

Newsletters from the temperance movement reveal that, in his twenties and following law school, my grandfather visited precisely 203 different college campuses around the country, speaking passionately about the evils of alcohol and the need for legally enforced prohibition of sales and consumption. He soon married my grandmother, Eva Piltz, a devout Methodist missionary, and began a family. She, like my grandfather, had been active in the temperance movement since her early teens. She devoted herself to their new family, maintaining the home while her husband worked exhaustively on behalf of the Prohibition movement.

In 1912, Virgil Sr. became chairman of the Prohibition National Committee, a post he held for a dozen years. During his tenure, the Eighteenth Amendment – the so-called Prohibition Amendment – was enacted, reflecting his skills at organization and persuasion, his political connections, and his relentless energy. Amazingly, Prohibition had become the law of the land.

He traveled extensively, both nationally and internationally. His visits to foreign countries were designed to promote the international Prohibition movement. During such journeys, he would often type lengthy letters to officials, relatives, and his sons late at night. Based on the pace of his travels, the expansiveness of his goals for worldwide temperance, his constant calculations and recalculations of mortgages on properties owned by his real estate clients, his energetic drive, and his expansive love for his family, he seems to have exhibited at least some hypomanic tendencies or traits. He did not, however, appear to suffer from any irrationality or despair. Indeed, recollections from relatives portray him as a determined man, whose faith and energy saw him through a large number of stressful life circumstances, yet who often showed gentleness in his demeanor and a warm twinkle in his eye. He summed up his optimism in a letter to his brother during the depths of the Great Depression, in the middle of the 1930s: "I never saw a day that I did not want to live a thousand years."

The firstborn son, my father's eldest brother Harold, was a tall, handsome boy. Born in 1912, he was the subject of high expectations from his parents. At an early age, however, and in defiance of the family pattern, he began to display delinquent behavior. Addicted to alcohol for most of his adult life, he held erratic jobs and died in his sixties, following a drinking binge.

The second brother, Randall (born in 1915), was less athletic and more introspective. At the age of seven, he had been with his two younger brothers when their mother's coffin was displayed in the living room, remembering their father's statement that they would not see her again. Later, as an adolescent, he was bedridden for nearly a year with rheumatic fever, reading extensively and shaping a longstanding interest in academic matters. He became an international economist of considerable repute. By nature both anxious and extremely generous, he was an anchor of stability among the family.

The third brother, Robert, born in 1918, was a year and a half older than my father. Tall, gregarious, and athletic, he was a close and competitive sibling to my father. He was stunned by the events that took place in my father's life during their adolescence and informed me, years later, that his career choice (he obtained both a doctorate in psychology and an M.D. prior to his training as a psychiatrist) was shaped largely by my father's mental illness. He was instrumental, in fact, in helping my father to secure treatment during later episodes. As an adult, however, he became addicted to painkillers, used initially to cope with his severe migraines, an affliction characterizing nearly all of the members of the family. He ultimately lost a leg from self-injection and later suffered from progressive renal failure. Well before his time, he died following kidney replacement surgery at the age of sixty.

Virgil Jr. was born late in 1919, and lost his mother in January 1923.

Following his father's remarriage, Junior subsequently gained two younger half-brothers, whom he helped to care for. The elder, Harvey, born in 1925, has had a career as a professor of music and an academic concert pianist, and the younger, Paul, born in 1927, is an accomplished tenor soloist. Each of them had first-born sons – my cousins and contemporaries – with extremely severe psychiatric problems.

Harvey's son, raised in the Midwest, had schizoaffective disorder, a condition marked by both manic and depressive mood swings and persistent, chronic thought disorder and paranoia in between the episodes. He lived in and out of mental hospitals and halfway houses during his twenties and committed suicide in the 1980s, not yet thirty years of age.

Paul's son developed schizophrenia early in college, during the late 1960s at the University of California, Berkeley. His

disorder began with severe disturbances of thinking, hallucinations and delusions, and erratic, irrational behavior. He has
had a chronic course of this disorder since that time. For the
past three decades he has endured multiple hospitalizations,
sporadic use of many different antipsychotic medications,
protracted stays in board-and-care residences, frequent home-
lessness, and an extremely marginal existence.

Across several generations, the family history on my father's
side has been marked by both high achievement and noteworthy mental disorder. To what might this "loaded" history be
compared? Some perspective may be gained by reading Kay
Redfield Jamison's book *Touched with Fire*, in which she describes a number of artistic and literary families with strong
histories of mental disorder.[1] For example, the nineteenth-
century Tennysons of Great Britain displayed an almost un-
believably strong blending of creativity and severe psychosis
both within and across generations. I note that, in my mother's
family, there is a weaker pattern of mental disorder, although
alcoholism and depression are present to some degree.

As I came to learn more about my father's family during
adolescence and young adulthood, I sometimes feared that I
was walking on eggshells, waiting for disaster to occur. As do
many individuals in such families, I wondered what I myself
might be "carrying." I made crude diagrams of the various
generations and their levels of affliction, mimicking the kinds
of pedigree charts found in primers of genetically transmitted
disorders. At the same time, I was also proud of, if daunted
by, the achievements of my extended "California" family. This
juxtaposition of accomplishment and attainment, on the one
hand, with despair and debilitation on the other, is another
bipolarity that surrounds families who have members afflicted
with mental disorder, particularly manic-depressive illness. It
certainly plagued me during many days of my young adulthood.

21

Speculating about the not-too-distant future, when more precise genetic markers of major mental illness are identified and more accurate percentages of personal or family risk for major mental disorders may be calculated, what new conflicts will emerge for family members – and for society at large? Potential advances in genetics and genomics (the study and practice of active gene manipulation) will probably cut both ways.[2] On the one hand, they may be liberating, to the extent that disabling neurological and psychiatric disorders may be detected, controlled, and possibly even prevented before the worst symptoms emerge. On the other, they may also serve to stigmatize and segregate persons at risk even further, with the specter of genetic "prevention" of many additional forms of mental disorder through abortion becoming a more prevalent option. But I am getting ahead of the story by considering these types of ethical issues, salient as they are in light of fast-breaking advances in the field. Back to my father's early years: How did he develop during his childhood in California?

2

Childhood and Adolescence

In the 1980s, by this time over sixty-five years of age, my father received a letter. The writer noted that he had found my father's name in Who's Who, *in the context of soliciting memories from people who grew up during the Great Depression. His aim was to discover the tenor and character of that era from those who had lived through it. The letter posed several questions about family hardships as well as personal meanings attached to events of the Depression; it also solicited my father's most salient memory of the period. My father kept a copy of his response in his files, from which I quote:*

As to hardships that occurred: Much could be said on this score. Of course we underwent hardships . . . yet since everyone we knew was likewise suffering the rigors of the times, it became a way of life for most of us. Your question (regarding perception of hardships) is a little like that of asking the people of the Dark Ages whether they knew they were living in the Dark Ages. Since, for the most part, they could not contrast their lives with the lives of those who lived before or after, they probably weathered the storm of ignorance and suffering without really knowing it. And likewise in my case of living during the Depression. All the brothers who could found jobs to help support themselves and the family before and after 1929. For the middle class, one might almost say that there was a kind of camaraderie *or close companionship in mild misery.*

Closely related is your next question: "How did the Depression change you, in attitude or way of life, or both?" Surely the austerity of the Depression helped shape me. Of necessity I engaged in self-restraint, self-denial, and self-control generally, and thus adopted a stark simplicity of life style. But even without the Depression, my daily regimen of school study, work, and athletics would have been quite similar because my Quaker father and former Methodist missionary stepmother reared me in a Christian manner to seek service to others as the goal of life. My father . . . served as my role model of Christian reformer, while my stepmother, who wanted me to be a medical missionary or minister, kept me "on the straight and narrow path" with serious religious training – with precepts instilled by much praise and regular corporal punishment.

Behind these measured words about his upbringing, however, lay a complicated history, with the reference to "regular corporal punishment" signaling a pattern of interchange between stepson and stepmother not shared by the rest of the household.

Junior began to attend elementary school in 1925, just after his first half-brother was born. In second grade he transferred to a John Dewey progressive school in Pasadena, several miles away. He would usually roller-skate to school, a daily event that he recalled, many years later, with considerable joy.

Family routines were well established: studying, religious training, and practicing and competing in athletics. The oldest brothers performed work around the neighborhood to aid with family income. As he matured into late childhood and early adolescence, Junior took on considerable responsibility for helping with his two younger half-brothers.

Childhood and Adolescence

Intellectually precocious, Junior also showed signs of defiance and wit. As described in a typed manuscript from his adulthood:

> Accustomed to stern discipline at home, I found the open classroom atmosphere at the progressive school a welcome change. I soon took advantage of this freedom by acting . . . as I would never dare to act at home in front of my (step)mother. In short, I soon became a smart alec. One day as I persisted in talking and laughing with my seat mates (in French class, which was taught in a more structured than open manner), our teacher became exasperated and said: "I don't like your attitude." Whereupon, quick as a wink, I stood up, climbed onto and stood on my desk top, and replied to her: "Well, how do you like my altitude?" The students laughed and, carried away by my spontaneous outburst, I was unconscious of my rudeness or at least of its possible long-run consequences. Little did I know. . . .

Junior was sent to the principal's office for his transgression, and the principal telephoned to the family home to report the misdeed. His stepmother took the call.

> When I got home the whole situation suddenly changed. . . . No one else was at home; so she seized that moment for purgative punishment. This spanking was surely the longest I had ever received. "We'll do this once a week until you have learned your lesson," she softly but sternly said. "Plan to be spanked, just like today, for the next three weeks. You may pick the day of the week and the time of the day." And so it was to be: I *asked* her for a spanking three more times.

By his early elementary school years, it was clear that Junior had formed a distinctive relationship with his stepmother. A heavy-set, pleasant-looking woman, she apparently saw in her youngest stepson the only one young and pliable enough to

25

raise in her own style, which was based on her strict discipline of the high-school girls who had been under her care in her role as principal of a missionary school. Upon marrying my grandfather, she secured a verbal promise that he would discipline the older boys, when he was home, but that she would be responsible for discipline of the youngest, Junior.

During this period, my grandfather was often away. After resigning as chairman of the Prohibition National Committee in 1924, he redoubled his travels to Washington, D.C., to Mexico, and to European capitals in order to promote the international prohibition movement. He took on the role of superintendent of the International Reform Foundation. When not traveling, he was engaged in numerous real estate transactions, attempting to fund the movement and provide for the family.

His expansive visions are exemplified in a statement he wrote for the international prohibition publication, *World Dry*, which conveyed his predictions for the year 1925. Following his statements about progress toward prohibition in Mexico, he wrote the following:

> Europe opens to us a field ripe for endeavor. The sixty-seven institutions of higher learning in Austria ... have inaugurated a movement for nation-wide Prohibition.... 200,000 signatures will be required.... 25,000 have already been secured and thousands more are being added each month.... We will make a great mistake if we do not co-operate to the utmost of our ability with those European nations which are trying so hard to make progress along the lines of Civic betterment. Much more can be done now, before conditions reach a settled state. When Europe becomes more prosperous again it will be more difficult to advance the work of moral reform....
>
> We face new opportunities in the home field. The work of securing legislation in Congress in behalf of the Child Labor Movement, uniform marriage and divorce laws.... demands

our immediate attention.... Not only do we face new opportunities, we face new problems. The world vision which possessed the minds of people of this country at the close of the war has in a great measure vanished.... This change of attitude on the part of the American people makes it exceedingly difficult to finance the most needed work abroad. The Bible says, "Cast your bread upon the waters and after many days it shall return," which might be interpreted, "Cast your surplus wealth for the world's moral and spiritual betterment in the greatest crisis of the ages and it will rebound to your uplift and progress." And if spoken to the United States Government, it might read, "Cast your billions which are worse than wasted for enlarged armament, in binding up the wounds of a broken world and there will return unto you ample protection of a more stable and lasting character than can be afforded by army and navy."

Apparent in such writing are his grand visions, his international scope, his meshing of biblical with political themes, his blending of prohibition with progressive causes (such as child labor reform), and his moral fervor.

Back in Pasadena, Junior's stepmother had high expectations for her youngest stepson's intellectual progress and his behavioral compliance. She often praised him to houseguests for his academic excellence and strong religious nature. She also enforced a strict regimen of discipline, as my father emphasized in lengthy pages of writings he made as an adult:

Freedom of speech was the first liberty I lost if the speech was the least bit impudent. Minor offenses were at first simply verbally corrected after a hard slap or two on each cheek. If such offenses were repeated, I would be asked to go to the bathroom and wait. Out would come the bar of soap and a wet wash cloth while my mother proceeded to vigorously wash out my mouth with soap. The actual washing was not so bad, but her righteous indignation and her

27

size (about five feet four inches tall, but over two hundred pounds in weight) made even such punishment frightening. . . . When I was a little older she gave up the soap for castor oil. . . . Greater offenses always merited spankings, always bare, at first in the bathroom downstairs and later in my bedroom upstairs. . . . The spankings were always hard and always hurt (about 15 to 20 spanks at first), yet even as a four year old I never cried during or after such discipline (as) a matter of pride, defiance, and masochism. . . .

What my father especially recalled was that, following a transgression, his stepmother asked him to go upstairs to his room and wait for the inevitable punishment.

As soon as I grew a little older the ritual became more formalized and more formidable. . . . Sometimes the wait in bed was short, sometimes long (an hour or more), but it usually seemed long. Her eyes and face were always very stern at such times, but her manner was that of a high school principal about to punish some tenth-grade girl for breaking rules. . . . She spoke calmly but with moral fervor, knowing that no infraction of rules she had laid down was to go unpunished. Finally there would be a summation of reasons for my guilt. At length, she would always ask: "Do you think you ought to be punished?" I would meekly assent. . . . I would then climb on the bed on my knees (in the punishment position). . . . In righteously indignant gestures, (she) proceeded with the inevitable – the rhythmic, hard handspanking. I can still vividly hear and feel the spank! spank! spank! of this and the many other spankings that were to follow.

Later, strapping replaced spanking:

I believe that it was the first time I was razor strapped that Mother suggested it would be better if I were tied when strapped so as to avoid injury from my involuntary movements while being whipped. . . . As her father, an upright,

German-American Methodist, had strapped her, now she must strap me. I am convinced she loved me deeply, and that she thought strapping was necessary to shape me into a good man.

My father wrote of his developing interest in self-punishment:

I began to take a keep interest . . . in seeing what happened to my flesh, on and near the buttocks, at the very moment I whipped myself with a belt . . . now and then I would strip, turn my buttocks toward the mirror, and proceed to strap myself while watching out of the corner of my eye. I became fascinated by the patterns of red stripes that would gradually appear across my white bottom.

She delivered other punishments that she referred to as purgative – for example, use of lengthy enemas. My father was aware of psychological aspects of the punishment rituals as well:

. . . feeling so vulnerable, waiting for the verdict of discipline, waiting for the sound spanking which inevitably followed . . . waiting, always waiting rather than getting it all over with. . . . Her disciplining me in private allowed license for what today might be called *child abuse*. In those days, however, her private rituals with me would probably have been considered just strict discipline that a step-mother might administer – at least by outsiders who knew few details of what went on.

(When I was young) Mother expressed some astonishment when, on being spanked in turn with my next-older brother (a year and a half older), I never cried or cried out even though he did. Later on, she commended me for neither crying nor crying out when she strapped me harder than she had her senior girls. Astonished though she might have been at my early stoicism, Mother frequently praised me for it, chiefly because, I have come to think, my silence insured even greater privacy since the on-going ritual of punishment was less likely to be overheard.

In the aftermath of some punishments, his next-oldest brother, Bob, would try to comfort him. Also, immediately after a particularly hard spanking or strapping, she herself would rub oil into his wounds, providing some relief. The ritual of spanking followed by soothing began to take on a sexualized flavor, as, during preadolescence, my father began to associate the relief from the cessation of spanking with sensual pleasure.

During some punishments, recalling her missionary days in Latin America, she would invoke Spanish to initiate the ritual:

"Presenteme, por favor, tus naglas desnudas para zurrate" or "Please present to me your nude buttocks so I may spank (or whip) you." "Immediatemente, Madre," I would reply.

Just before my father reached the age of ten, the stock market crash of October 1929 occurred, and the family underwent many changes. My grandfather's Prohibition-related efforts were markedly curtailed, and many of the properties he owned or managed were lost. He often wrote to relatives during this period, documenting his worries about increasing debts and his valiant attempts to hold on to the remaining properties. He maintained optimism throughout this period, however, and the family was able to keep their home. To do so, the boys were increasingly forced to find whatever work they could after school hours. My father wrote the following:

(In late elementary school) I had mostly gardening jobs, the first paying $17\frac{1}{2}$ cents per hour. I was fortunate to be able to keep these jobs as times got worse in the early 30's. Later I was an iceman's helper on a route with 600 stops, at least on Saturdays ... (and later) a student secretary at Pasadena

Junior College hired with National Youth Administration funds (at 40 cents an hour), and a chauffeur for an elderly lady. As a real estate broker and lawyer, my father lost all clients. The family thus went on W.P.A. (Works Progress Administration). This meant that for manual labor my father was paid in food, not money. An uncle, who had been a fireman, lost his job and made ends meet by delivering small newspapers in South Pasadena.

At one dinnertime, my father recalled, the boys were polled to see if anyone had any money for dinner. Junior, alone, had a dime in his pocket, which funded the evening meal.

During his school years, my father not only studied hard but enjoyed athletics. A muscular boy who grew to just under six feet tall, he participated in football, baseball, and track and field. Newspaper clippings from the 1930s include pictures and stories about him as regional shotput champion in tenth grade. Relatives recall the regular practice for this sport that he performed in the small backyard and driveway of the family home, the shotput wearing a hole in the ground near the landing area next to the garage. In junior high, he had been squad captain for a group that included the young Jackie Robinson, the first African-American to play major league baseball some years later. "I taught Jackie everything he knew about sports," my father jokingly told me in later life.

The household witnessed intense discussion of current issues, and a number of foreign and domestic visitors, chiefly related to the Prohibition movement, often stayed at the house to discuss religious and political topics. Competitive sparring over academic attainment was a daily event; religious training was a mainstay of family activities. As the youngest of the original four boys, my father was often the victim of rough-house play. Yet he also used his brothers' advanced years as an impetus to compete, both athletically and academically. As

31

an example of the nature of the interactions among the brothers, my father recalled to me his family's teasing him about proceeding from high school to Pasadena *Junior* College and then to Leland Stanford, *Junior*, University. His brothers asked him, "When will you ever go to a real school, Junior?!"

During the time that he attained puberty and began to show interest in girls, his stepmother's punishments increased in intensity. Caught kissing a neighbor girl in the sixth grade, Junior was ritually spanked and strapped by his stepmother, who also spanked the girl and reported the incident to her father. At age fifteen, he later recalled, his stepmother provided a final, extremely harsh punishment when she became suspicious of his further interest in girls, a punishment that included strapping, soothing, and enema purging. This was the last punishment that she delivered, however, as Junior had by this time attained full adolescence. Yet the memory of such discipline at the hands of his stepmother stayed with him throughout his life.

3

Breakdown and Recovery

Handwritten recollections, made almost fifty years later, of my father's state of mind during his first hospitalization, at age sixteen:

(a) *At one with the world – "in, but not of, this world"*

(b) *Celestial music of the spheres, all night long, since I slept so little*

(c) *In the Hallway of Hell, with micro- and macrocephalics, "torchered" soul of the damned, draped on wire enclosures*

(d) *Being beaten with short mop handles, especially on the head, losing consciousness, falling on the floor and being "revived"*

(e) *Getting up early to join the garbage team work crew*

(f) *Tried to relive my own infancy and childhood, or the infancy of Vergil, the Roman Poet, especially as to the learning of language. Likewise, to probe the origin of all language, from the baby Vergil's/Virgil's first word. Are many of the Latin words echoic in origin, and related to the breathing patterns of a baby? Was I, in some respects, the Vergil of the Aeneid? Is there metempsychosis? Reincarnation?*

The chain of events began in the sultry heat of the late summer in Southern California, during sleepless, agitated nights when thoughts of incipient death and war in Europe jumbled together in my father's mind. Following what seems, with hindsight, to be an inevitable progression, he became sufficiently confused and self-destructive that he nearly took his own life. His "treatment" was to be warehoused in a county facility, tied to his bed to thwart his agitation. The self-destruction did not stop, however, as he refused food out of the delusional fear that it was poisoned. Only after many months did he quickly and nearly spontaneously recover. These events severely shook the family and forever altered Junior's fundamental ways of viewing himself and the world.

In August 1936, Junior was preparing for the scheduled start of twelfth grade at Pasadena Junior College. At that time in Pasadena and in much of California, high school ended in tenth grade, with a four-year regimen of junior college immediately afterward, before the final two-year period of university education.

He began to have trouble, however, sleeping through the night. Floating through his mind were thoughts about the world situation, particularly in Western Europe. European visitors to the family home had told of ominous events in Nazi Germany, with many voicing the opinion that Hitler's military preparations would, in fact, ensure Nazi domination of not only Europe but the entire world in the inevitable conflicts to come. The scholarliness of the family, and their international contacts, made them far less "isolationist" than much of the country during the 1930s, providing fertile soil for Junior's ruminations.

Increasingly agitated and suspicious, and full of such thoughts, Junior hardly slept for a period of several days in early September. Although his energy level was high, his thinking was morbid and full of doom. In psychiatric terms, he was exhibiting signs of a "mixed state," blending the high energy level of mania with the depressive, self-destructive ruminations of depression. The Nazi threat became increasingly magnified as his mind raced toward chaos. He wondered what he might be able to do in order to make some kind of statement regarding the world situation, as the clouds in his mind darkened and his judgment became increasingly poor.

On September 6, having spent the previous Saturday night walking through the streets of Pasadena, with his family now worried about his appearance and behavior, he approached the house in the morning, the hot sun intensifying his agitation. His thoughts were jumbled: Shouldn't I soon be going to church, as the family did each Sunday? Why doesn't everyone realize what sacrifices need to be made if Hitler is to be countered?

As he neared the house, he shed his clothes. Upon attaining the yard, he climbed up the side of the porch to the roof. With the delusion that he could fly, and with grand thoughts of making a statement that Hitler and fascism can and must be stopped, he jumped to the yard and walkway below.

Startled by the commotion and wondering where Junior had been, the family rushed out. What was he doing unclothed and bleeding, sprawled in the yard? Although physical injuries were luckily minor, police officers and a cousin (a woman physician) were called in, certifying his "insanity" and taking him, shackled, to the large county hospital some miles away.

After a legal hearing two weeks later, Junior was placed in another public facility, a county hospital for those with psychiatric illnesses or feeblemindedness, the term of the era for mental retardation. At that point in the Depression, the family had no money for a private hospital. What were his thoughts, I have often wondered, as he was transferred to the county institution? Although he could not precisely recall, in later years, the transfer itself, he maintained vivid memories of his lengthy stay at the second facility.

Housed in this hospital were a variety of psychotic and mentally retarded individuals who shared a propensity for chaotic behavior and a pervasive lack of hope. He often commented, later in life, on sharing a ward with "macro- and micro-encephalics" – individuals whose organically based brain disorders led to distorted head shapes and sizes as well as mental retardation. His self-image, in fact, appears to have merged with such visibly disfigured persons. Among his more vivid recollections were the constant screaming and the punishments that included being tied to the bed for agitated behavior. Whether his specific recollection of being beaten with mop handles, excerpted in his writings at the beginning of this chapter, was real or delusional, I cannot say.

During the initial period of his hospitalization, he was quite agitated and paranoid. Soon, he began to refuse all food, related to the delusional belief that anything he ate would contaminate him. He began to shed weight, leading to drastic reductions in his size, eventually losing over fifty pounds from his muscular frame.

Much of his thinking was taken up by religious themes, as indicated by his recollections ("celestial music of the spheres, all night long"). He was self-destructive and irrational, nearly losing his life from his refusal to eat. The relatively quick transition from student/athlete to inmate, and his resultant confusion, chaos, terror, and fear are scarcely imaginable.

The family was greatly distressed, wondering what had brought Junior into such a state. Religious faith helped to contain the fears. His older brothers were shocked and devastated, finding it hard to believe that their bright, athletic, and enthusiastic sibling had sunk into such chaos and irrationality in so short a period of time.

My grandfather revealed some of his reactions during this period in a letter he sent to his brother several years after this episode. The main purpose of the letter was to console this brother, whose daughter – a first cousin of my father's – had suddenly died in her late twenties, following a history of emotional disorder, eating difficulties, and depression. It is not clear, in fact, whether her death was suicidal. Virgil Sr. tried to empathize, given his experiences with Junior:

> Of course I have not gone through with just what you are going through. I came the nearest with Junior. When (in 1936) he fell off from 173 to 121 pounds in 3 weeks, and we were called in to the hospital and told by the head physician that he might go at any time, I came home fully reconciled to the most probable fate. In other words he became for the time being as one who had left permanently. I did not see how he could recover. From a philosophical point of view we have but a few years ahead if we do not outlive our ancestors, and we have not long to grieve over anything, and if life is eternal as I fully believe it is, we will soon meet those who have gone before....

Late in the fall, Junior's condition began to improve, at first gradually. He started eating, slowly regaining weight and taking himself out of imminent physical danger. Yet his thinking was still severely disordered. He continued to hear voices and continued to seek ultimate truths about the nature of his strange, preoccupied beliefs. As the fall turned into winter, he wished fervently for a return home in time for the Christmas holiday. Yet he was still too ill to be discharged. Bitterly disappointed, he remained in the facility. No therapy was offered.

By February, however, his mood rather suddenly stabilized and the hallucinations and delusions cleared. As was the case during many subsequent episodes and hospitalizations, this phase of improvement, once it began, was rapid and apparently spontaneous, following months of severe disorganization and self-destructive behavior. His release from the hospital came in several weeks. His physical as well as emotional strength had fully reappeared.

Once back home, with a clear mind and with little motivation to dwell on the previous half year, he was driven to recoup his losses. In fact, he completed his entire twelfth-grade curriculum that spring, in less than a semester, maintaining his A average. The family was greatly relieved to witness his return to normal functioning, although the juxtaposition seemed almost unreal. What could have happened? they continued to ask themselves. Clearly, their faith had been rewarded by Junior's recovery, but the family's sense of stability had been permanently shaken.

Neither follow-up psychiatric care nor counseling for readjustment was provided to Junior or the family. Such measures simply did not exist at the time, at least with discharge from public facilities. Although formal records are not available, schizophrenic psychosis was the diagnosis given, as revealed in subsequent diagnoses he received.

During the next two years, Junior continued with his junior college curriculum, earning top grades. His recovery was sustained and complete. He became a skillful orator in school, succeeding and earning awards in regional and even national competitions. As Virgil Sr. wrote to relatives at the time:

> Boys all doing well in school. Junior has been elected to 3 scholarship societies and has served as toast master at 2 banquets the past week where scholarship societies met.

During his last year of junior college, with a stellar academic record, he applied to college and was awarded scholarships to both Stanford and the University of California, Berkeley. He later told me, on many occasions and always with delight, that he remembered the day that his full year's scholarship for Berkeley arrived in the mail. Covering the entire year's fees, the check totaled $75!

Breakdown and Recovery

He graduated as valedictorian of his junior college class, speaking at the Rose Bowl on graduation day in front of thousands of listeners. He returned the check to the University of California, instead choosing Stanford. He became further attracted to philosophy while studying there, supporting himself by holding various jobs: serving a hasher in an eating club, a gardener for a psychology professor, and an employee of the main campus library. Attracted to the study of the mind, the quest for human knowledge, and the ethical and metaphysical dilemmas posed by the great philosophers, he double-majored in philosophy and psychology.

The famous Stanford chapel was always one of his favorite spots, reminding him of his religious training. Indeed, pronounced religiosity and the constant speaking of Spanish (the language brought by his stepmother from her Methodist missionary days) marked the early stages of many of his later episodes.

My grandfather wrote to his brother again in 1940, commenting once more on his sons' accomplishments. His calm words understate his pride:

> The boys are now home ... tomorrow evening we will have our annual Christmas Eve gathering of some forty to fifty people.... Junior just received his grades from Stanford. For the past quarter, he got 4 A grades and one B. The first quarter he got all A grades. He has a lot of work on the side.

In the summer of 1941, Virgil Sr. wrote again, this time of his recent trip to Northern California with his wife to attend Junior's graduation from Stanford:

> There were ten thousand present from various parts of the land. There were 878 in his senior class, and they were divided into three groups: 1. Those who got diplomas with no notice of superiority. 2. Those who got Phi Beta Kappa. 3. Those who ... had, in their diplomas, the degree

of Bachelor of Arts with Great Distinction. There were 79 in the second class, 41 in the third class, and all the others in the first class. Junior was in both the second and third class. He now has a job for the summer with his truck delivering ice....

Junior faced several choices. His father wished that that he remain in Southern California to help with various Quaker causes – for example, international meetings regarding famine relief overseas. Junior also contemplated, briefly, taking a graduate business course at Stanford. But he realized that his calling was philosophy.

He was accepted at the University of Iowa, where he studied the following year, earning a one-year Master's degree in philosophy and psychology and working under the mentorship of Gustav Bergman, a member of the Vienna Circle of European philosophers and refugee from Hitler's Europe. Any disappointment my grandfather may have had in Junior's decision to study philosophy was quickly forgotten.

My father was viewed as one of the most promising graduate students in the field. He was greatly influenced by logical positivism, the philosophical system that attempted to place human knowledge in the grounding of verifiable data from the senses and formal logical principles. Yet he was also quite taken with the Freudian theory about which he had begun to read. He applied for doctoral study at Princeton and was accepted with a fellowship. His academic career was ascending, with the chaos and hospitalization of mid-adolescence receding farther into the background.

4

Professorship and Family

It is the winter of 1945. The newly degreed Dr. Hinshaw has com-
pleted his doctoral dissertation, an important piece of philosophical
scholarship dealing with the theory of knowledge, the basis of
people's information about the world. World War II is nearing its
final stages, at least in Europe, with the Battle of the Bulge now
completed and the Allied drive to Germany gaining increasing
certainty. For a twenty-five-year-old with such credentials and at
such a time, the world could only appear to be a most promising
place. Hitler will soon be vanquished, and an academic career
appears to be there for the taking.

But agitation and paranoia suddenly recur. Virgil has become
romantically involved with a woman he has met at Princeton,
wishing to marry her, but she cannot make the choice to become
his partner. He becomes despondent, then angry and confused
over the loss. Hurt, and with growing suspicion and a sense of
entitlement, he takes the train to New York City, where she lives.
He rings her bell and knocks at her door, but no one responds. He
continues knocking with increased intensity. Panicked and by
now nearly delusional, he shouts up at her window in the cold
winter night. Neighbors become alarmed and call the police.

A familiar scene recurs: booking, psychiatric evaluation, the
decision to institutionalize. He again ends up in a psychiatric

hospital, this time in Philadelphia, the closest public facility to Princeton. Once again he is irrational, paranoid, agitated, and chaotic; once more he is locked up. Despite the passage of eight and a half years since his first hospitalization, there are still no specific treatments for this kind of madness. Rather, he is sedated with barbiturates, kept on the ward, left to deal with his agitation and confusion largely alone, except for the company of his fellow inmates. On several occasions he receives insulin "shock" therapy, an early variant of electroconvulsive therapy in which seizures are induced by large dosages of insulin, in the hope of eliminating or tempering the voices, delusions, and chaotic behavior.

The war effort, with rationing in place, serves to diminish his family's efforts to find him better care. Indeed, they are 3,000 miles away, across the continent.

On a Sunday during his hospital stay, a large number of patients attend Catholic mass. It is the only religious service available, and he goes, too. Reflecting the impulsivity and sexual preoccupation that are characteristic of his state, he believes that it would be both funny – similar to the dorm humor of his under-graduate days, as he later recounted – and blasphemous to make a loud and sexually crude interpretation of what the priest was doing to the assembled worshippers. Following his shouted comment, however, no one else shares the humor. Many of the other patients, in particular, are far from amused.

Later that afternoon several peers strike him hard in the face. That evening, as he wrote many years later on his manual typewriter:

When the new shift of attendants was about to come on duty at 10 p.m., I was rudely awakened. A group of patients ... abruptly escorted me to a far back room used for occupational therapy ... leading me over to a slightly worn gymnastic horse. Immedi-ately I sensed, as in a deja vu of my (step)Mother's stern but loving routine for major punishment with a razor strap, the sound thrashing I was about to undergo. ... As I had learned

42

from my Mother, failure to obey at this juncture would only increase the intensity or length of the punishment, or both.

The whipping takes place. In his mind, the circle was complete: His earlier punishments are now replayed, in terms of both his hospitalization and now the confrontation by fellow patients. Why resist? The punishments are part of his identity, and compliance is the only choice.

The hospitalization drags on for five more months, not the kind of graduation that the newly titled Dr. Hinshaw had anticipated.

With conscientious objector status conferred because of both his Quaker background and a record of mental hospitalization during adolescence, Junior began doctoral studies at Princeton's graduate school in the fall of 1941, where he was awarded a University Fellowship. His two next-oldest brothers were also attending this exclusive graduate school in their respective fields, Randall in economics and Bob in psychology, and the three brothers overlapped in their studies for a period of time. Although still "Junior" to them, he was known as Virgil or Mr. Hinshaw to the rest of the world.

Princeton was home to a stunning array of scholars at that time. The renowned British philosopher Bertrand Russell was a visitor there during Virgil's initial year of graduate study. The philosophy department arranged that Virgil have weekly tea at Russell's home, where he relished the philosophical discussions. Among others he encountered were Kurt Gödel, creator of the uncertainty theorem, and Richard Feynman, then a graduate student in physics. Betraying the practical orientation for which he was known, Feynman acidly commented to Virgil about the futility of philosophy as a viable enterprise.[1]

America was now officially part of World War II. Virgil divided time between his studies and working for the war effort, loading supply boxes to be sent overseas and helping with Civil Defense activities. He reconciled this war-related work with his Quaker upbringing through his strong commitment to stopping Hitler and fascism.

Although interested in all aspects of philosophy, from the Greek classics to modern logic, he was most excited about the basis and limits of scientific knowledge. He published several single-authored works in philosophy journals on theory of knowledge and philosophy of science during his graduate years, earning himself a name in the field.[2] By 1944, he began to devote full energy to writing his doctoral dissertation, entitled "An Inquiry into the Factual Basis of Human Knowledge." The work received high praise. Upon its completion, his potential appeared to be limitless. Yet almost immediately, as the words at the beginning of this chapter indicate, his mind began to unravel.

In recalling the period around the time of his hospitalization, he later wrote:

> Telekinesis; telepathy: spy abilities (cf. World War II atmosphere compared to world-wide fascism and Marxism of 1936) – fixate on license plate and not only memorize it but "transmit" it through ESP to nearest security (military, police, etc.). All this, of course, before taking (by hospital authorization) any medication or insulin/ECTtherapy...cf. my activity at Princeton as an aircraft identifier and reporter (by phone) to Civil Defense Headquarters.... Is telekinesis possible without being "off one's rocker"?

Clearly, the war effort permeated his illogical thinking, as he began to believe that he possessed special telekinetic powers that might, once again, stop fascism.

Randall had completed his doctorate in economics the previous year and was now working in Washington, D.C., for the war effort. As Virgil's hospitalization in Philadelphia progressed throughout the spring of 1945, Randall visited during each weekend that he could obtain a leave. Many years later, Randall recounted to me that his brother often had the delusion that he was being housed in a concentration camp in Europe. Indeed, when Virgil eventually got passes on weekends to leave the grounds, Randall would walk with him or, if fortunate enough to have access to a car and ration cards, take him on a drive. Virgil immediately translated any roadsigns into German, fueling the concentration camp delusion, fearing his and his brother's demise.

As Virgil began to show signs of improvement, Randall pleaded with his brother to cooperate with the staff and to drop his oppositional, paranoid stance, in order to facilitate discharge. Yet my father continued to hold irrational beliefs and to hear voices for several more months.

By summer, the symptoms began to clear rapidly, once again without much warning. The staff considered his discharge.

The war in Europe was now over, although it was uncertain how long the confrontation with Japan in the Pacific would last. Through the War Office in Washington, Randall arranged for the two brothers to take a train across the country back to the family home in California, following Virgil's discharge. He was able to obtain, however, only a single sleeper berth in the train crowded with soldiers returning from Europe, which the brothers shared. The train was packed, and it was hot, but victory was in the air and Virgil was in fine spirits.

It was mid-July as the train crossed northern New Mexico, and Randall read in the newspaper of the first test of an atomic bomb in Alamogordo, further down in the state, presaging the destruction of Hiroshima and Nagasaki and the end of the war, several weeks later. The train neared California, and Virgil's recovery had become complete. Indeed, he began to appear in nearly perfect physical and mental health. Randall himself, however, was nearly a wreck (as he later described himself) from the stress related to witnessing Virgil's hospitalization and traveling on the crowded train in the summer heat. When they finally arrived in Pasadena, according to Randall, anyone seeing the brothers would have guessed that it was he and not Virgil who had spent the previous five months in a mental hospital.

With his own recovery now in place, Virgil once again adjusted quickly to having a clear mind. He worked at various jobs in California, sending out applications for teaching positions. On his manual typewriter he produced cogent, articulate letters to department chairs, which he sent along with his academic resume. Apparently, no one inquired about his months out of commission. His academic trajectory had weathered the lost half-year in the hospital, and he eventually received several offers. He accepted an instructorship in philosophy at Ohio State, moving to Columbus in 1946 to begin his long affiliation with the university.

At this, his first academic job, he was bound and determined to succeed. His work continued to be brilliant, and he was productive. After a year, he was appointed to the rank of assistant professor, with the opportunity to obtain tenure if his scholarship and teaching continued to meet academic standards.

Colleagues recall his brilliant writings, lectures, and conference presentations during his initial years as well as his key role in upgrading the philosophy department into the world of formal logic and closer ties with the hard sciences. He helped to consolidate a monthly salon of interdisciplinary talks, across departments, which continues to this day. He worked energetically, teaching both Introduction to Philosophy and undergraduate and graduate seminars on metaphysics, theory of knowledge, philosophy of science, and philosophy of history. He continued to publish influential works in scholarly journals, probing the basis of human knowledge.

A close colleague of my father's noted that, in the late 1940s, when Virgil gave academic talks at regional and national conferences, heads would turn in the audience, as the listeners grasped the brilliance of his words and the spirit that infected them. This colleague also noted that, even in later years, when my father's intellectual drive and functioning had waned, he could still, when asked, give an impromptu and virtuoso talk on nearly any aspect of philosophy. His training had been both broad and deep; his mind was incandescent.

During the late 1940s, Virgil was invited back to Princeton for meetings with Albert Einstein at the Institute for Advanced Studies. From these encounters he prepared a paper on Einstein's social philosophy and moral sense, which appeared as the final chapter in a compendium of commentaries on the great physicist.[3]

During this time Virgil was introduced on a blind date to my mother, who had completed her graduate work at Ohio State in history. During their courtship, she recalls, he was both energetic and fun-loving and quite serious about his scholarship and career. He was the "apple of the department's eye," according to her, given his productivity and collegiality. He mentioned to her only in passing, however, the difficult times at Princeton and in Pasadena, failing to mention anything specific about hospitalizations or psychoses. As their relationship progressed, for the next two years, she was ignorant of his history.

The couple was married on June 12, 1950, in a formal ceremony in Columbus. Virgil was thirty years of age, and Alene was twenty-five. For their honeymoon, they drove cross-country. My mother recalls her thrill at seeing the American West for the first time. They were both clearly excited over their marriage and very much in love. They spent some time in Pasadena with Virgil's family. For him, it was a familiar scene, resuming the intellectual conversations with his brothers, who had gathered in Pasadena for the arrival of the newlyweds. Yet for my mother it was a source of bewilderment and amazement to hear and experience the competitive, sharp-witted repartee of the dinner table conversations with her new in-laws and the "boys." Who had outdone the other this past year? Who could one-up the rest by winning an argument? She befriended several of her sisters-in-law, who filled her in on the family's dynamics. She was thus introduced to the family, far different from her own Midwestern family of origin. Still, however, my mother did not learn any specifics of my father's episodes or hospitalizations. They drove back taking a more northerly route, after stopping in San Francisco, arriving in Columbus for married life.

The Ohio State campus and faculty colleagues were the focus of the couple's social life. Parties with friends from various departments, home football games at the huge stadium home of the powerhouse Buckeyes, evening events that included monthly playreading groups, badminton and volleyball games in the backyard – all filled the social calendar. Indeed, just a few years later, as a small boy, I experienced some of the parties and can still recall them vividly: the smell and sight of cocktails being served, the loud laughter of good friends convening in the family home, my father smoking his pipe with an infectious grin. I can still feel the inner thrill as the lights came on in the living room while the parties would extend from late afternoon until nighttime.

In private moments, however, Virgil revealed undercurrents of his upbringing. One night, early in their married life, he asked my mother to tie him up in bed, stating that this was what his stepmother had done to him when he was a boy. Shocked, my mother replied that she was not his stepmother, nor his keeper, but rather his wife. She was just beginning to realize the complexity and difficulty of this man. Most of her friends had married high-school sweethearts from the local area, she reflected years later; she hardly knew what she was getting into with this brilliant and captivating but also troubled husband.

Still, she held out hope for her new marriage. On a second driving trip to California, in the summer of 1952, my mother was pregnant with me. After staying at the family home in Pasadena once again, and visiting with all the relatives, my parents left Southern California for a drive up the coast, soon to return to Ohio. But on their first night out, at a motel near Santa Barbara, Virgil received a telephone message with tragic news. His father had been killed that same day when the car in which he was a passenger had, ironically, been hit by a drunk driver en route to Bakersfield. He had died at the age of seventy-six, still working and still in excellent health. My parents diverted their trip, driving many miles inland that night to identify the body. My mother recalls that my father coped with the loss with appropriate shock and sadness but without signs of disorganization or irrationality.

During the fall, following their return to Ohio and during the late stages of the pregnancy, Virgil began to display early signs of disturbance. He was overly jovial and overly energetic; his thinking processes soon became irrational. The episode was relatively short-lived, however, and hospitalization was not required. Still, during the late fall, he was not fully "there" for my mother, in terms of emotional support.

On December 1, 1952, a day that had brought a light snow to Columbus, my mother was admitted to the hospital to begin the birthing process. A complication developed: The umbilical cord became wrapped around my leg during the nighttime delivery, cutting off oxygen before I could breathe on my own. I was therefore blue at birth. The doctors intervened immediately, placing me in an incubator, where I ended up staying for eight days. Although I didn't appear to be in imminent danger, it was clearly an anxious time for my mother.*

My mother's obstetrician knew of her exhausted state and of the worry she was experiencing; he also knew that my father wasn't at full capacity. As head of the department at the hospital, he authorized my mother's extended stay for the full period that I was in intensive care. My mother was greatly relieved to be close by me, with an opportunity for rest. It is hard to imagine, in our current era of managed health care, that any such arrangement could be made today.

Mother and son soon went home, and the new parents were thrilled and proud, settling into the exhausting routine of nighttime awakenings and round-the-clock care. Virgil once again appeared stable mentally. Within five months, my mother became pregnant again. In the summer and fall of 1953, however, during this pregnancy with my sister, he became acutely symptomatic. Sleeplessness, paranoia, irrational thoughts, hallucinations, and delusions ensued; a full-blown episode was in place. He had to be hospitalized, and electroconvulsive therapy (ECT) was given, in which seizures are induced by sending an electric current through the brain. Bob, his psychiatrist brother, flew to Columbus to accompany my father to California for extended hospitalization. In February 1954, my mother gave birth to my sister, Sally, in the absence of my father, who was still hospitalized at the time. Relatives had to assist with my caretaking during this period.

---

* Much later I learned that my incubator had contained an enriched mixture of oxygen and nitrogen, in approximately equal parts. Just a year before, friends of my parents in Columbus had a boy who required incubation. Although he survived, he was rendered permanently blind. At that time, pure oxygen had been used for incubation, with the side effect in some cases of permanent damage to the retina. Only the passage of a few months of medical research enabled me to survive infancy with my eyesight.

Professorship and Family

My father returned within several months, again fully recovered following a prolonged period of extreme disorganization, agitation, irrational functioning, and hospitalization, to a house with two small children. The daily routines of childrearing resumed, as did his teaching at Ohio State. Discussion of his episode or absence did not take place, but the couple was once again intact. My mother recalls long days and nights, sterilizing bottles and caretaking little Stevie and Sally. Both she and Virgil adored the children, and matters at home had once again stabilized, if the task of raising two small children can ever be called stable.

But the long decade of the 1950s was far from over.

5

The '50s: An
Uphill Battle

It is the spring of 1958, and I am in kindergarten. I do not know that my mother and father had driven to Cincinnati in the middle of the night the previous fall, as described in the opening of Chapter 1. I do not know, either, that my father has been hospitalized several times during this decade, that he has received ECT, that he has been one of the initial patients in the country to be placed on Thorazine (chlorpromazine), the first antipsychotic medication ever used, which had been brought over from France several years before. Indeed, I did not learn of any of these events until many years later.

At age five, however, I have a different worry. It is about a fact that I have learned. I cannot now recall where I learned of this fact – perhaps on television, perhaps in a book or almanac. It must be true, given that I had seen or heard it, but I cannot seem to comprehend it.

I walk downstairs to the basement of our first house, the colonial-style home across the river from campus. My father's study is there, always cool and musty in its basement location. His books – the many books on philosophy, history, arts, math – line the walls. The books give a reddish-brown tint to the room, smelling faintly of the dampness of the basement. They signify, to me, how much there is to learn. Although the study has a makeshift feel, with cinderblocks serving as many of the book-shelves, it is my father's sanctuary.

He is reading, writing notes on a yellow legal pad, using his fountain pen, his elegant strokes filling the page. I ask to interrupt, as the fact I have learned is bothering me. Ever patient, he smiles at me and asks what I need.

I tell him that I can't understand something I've heard and read. He must sense the puzzlement on my face. "What could that be?" he gently inquires.

"Well, it says that Russia is the biggest country on earth in land" – by this, I mean in area – "and I think that this must be right. But they also say that China has more people than Russia, a bigger population. Is that really true? How could it be?" Clearly, the concept is beyond my comprehension.

My father explains that yes, it is actually true. He begins to discuss how more people could crowd together in a smaller area. I can't quite hear his explanation, however, because another, even more pressing question has now entered my mind, which I must ask before he has finished.

"If it's true," I interrupt, "then how many more people live in China than Russia?" I am searching for some way to quantify this incredible state of affairs.

"A great many more," my father replies, pausing for me to take this in.

I think for a while, then dare to ask the most puzzling question of all: "Could there be a hundred *more people living in China than in Russia?"*

With infinite patience and without a hint of bemusement, he responds gently: "Son, I know that this will be hard to believe, but there are actually more *than 100 more people living in China than Russia."*

My amazement has peaked, and I try to absorb this onslaught of information.

Even then, I was soothed by his patience and gentleness in answering me. Today, knowing of the decade, I am sometimes staggered.

M y father's episodes were intensifying in number and severity during the 1950s.

What were the initial signs? Initially, I have since learned, he would show classic symptoms of what is termed hypomania, the earliest stage of the full manic cycle. Sights and sounds were vivid and sensuous, a state of affairs termed hyperacusis, the intensification of sensory awareness. In addition, his speech became fast-paced and pressured, with punning and word games quickly emerging. He would begin to converse in Spanish, the language of his missionary stepmother, the language in which she would often ask him to wait for punishments. He also required much less sleep than usual, as though his internal engine was idling at a much higher rate than normal. He began to think grand thoughts and make major plans; in clinical terms, he was euphoric, expansive, and grandiose. He became sexually preoccupied. Also, religious thoughts and visions took over his mind. As I noted earlier, he began to play religious choral music on the phonograph, with the volume turned up far too loud.

Sometimes his episode would go no further than this set of symptoms, that is, it would peak at the phase of hypomania for a number of weeks and then recede. As best I can determine, such mild episodes might last several months from beginning to end.

More frequently, however, he would "progress" to more advanced stages of mania after a period of hypomanic symptoms, with the emergence of symptoms that were far more severe. For one thing, he would become impulsive, deciding quickly to follow through with an idea, however unrealistic, signaling a clear loss of judgment. His mood would become quite irritable, especially if he was "crossed" in the planning of his ventures or if he felt thwarted in any way. In addition, he was prone to experiencing mysterious and troubling "ideas of reference." These involve the reading of special, personalized meanings into everyday events, like his perception of the singer's conveying messages to him over the airwaves from Cincinnati.

After some period of time, such ideas of reference would crystallize into frank paranoia, in which a whole system of strange, aberrant beliefs would emerge. At these times, hallucinations (often, for my father, hearing voices) and delusions (the presence of bizarre, fixed beliefs that are greatly at odds with most people's conceptions of reality) would emerge. As if this escalation weren't enough, he would often proceed (or rather, deteriorate) even further into deeper realms of mania, in which the psychotic symptoms (rampant hallucinations and delusions, extreme disorganization of behavior, utter agitation) would become sufficiently chaotic that hospitalization was the only real option. During much of the last century, such psychotic behavior patterns were believed to signify schizophrenia, the diagnosis he carried with him (see Chapter 7). Today, however, the consensus is that if mania progresses beyond its initial stage, psychotic functioning routinely emerges.

Back to the initial days and weeks: Early warning signs in my father could be subtle but chilling. My mother recalls, on one occasion, waiting at the airport for him while he was flying home after an out-of-town philosophy conference. Waiting at the gate, she saw him deplane and walk toward the terminal. Once he was inside and made eye contact, she immediately noticed a particular glint in his eye as he approached her. Her knees reflexively weakened with fear as she realized that an utterly irrational, paranoid, psychotic episode was inevitable. Knowing what would be coming, and without power to stop its course, she was nearly sick with anticipation and dread.

She told me years later that it was as though she could sense a chemical change inside him, which blew through her like an ill wind. Given what the field knows today about biochemical changes that may accompany the sometimes sudden "switch" into mania, her intuition seems distinctly on target.[1]

Her family in the area, particularly her mother, had no real understanding of mental illness, and she thus needed to "cover" both his episodes and their aftereffects as best she could. In retrospect, the effort seems nearly superhuman.

Even when in the throes of full-blown mania, however, and clearly irrational, my father rarely, if ever, acted out in front of my sister or me. Somehow, he would maintain some control, some sense of boundary, with tremendous aid from my mother, who diverted him from the children at such times. Such masking and control are not an indication that his symptoms were volitional but rather that both my father and mother maintained strong motivation to contain the out-of-control behaviors – and somehow managed to do so.

And once he was hospitalized, or once an episode had ended and he had returned home, there was simply no further discussion or conversation. His absences hung in the air like a brittle, fragile bubble containing poison, off-limits for fear of toxic release. I still wonder about the cost of "sitting on" these kinds of experiences. The fear that their disclosure would taint any relationship and serve to fuel even more distance and revulsion must have been overwhelming.

Although I know of no other specifics, during one episode – which had clearly progressed to an advanced stage of mania – my father went into the backyard and, one by one, broke his golf clubs in a rage, snapping them over his knee and heaving the pieces into neighbors' yards. Who knows what set off this rage? Perhaps he felt thwarted that others (his wife, friends, colleagues) couldn't keep pace with his frantic energy or his unrealistic, grandiose plans. It goes without saying that breaking golf clubs is no easy feat; the hostility of his negative energy must have been considerable. An enthusiastic golfer before that time, he rarely played the game again.

When he was functioning normally, however, during his often protracted periods of stable mood (termed "euthymia") between episodes, nearly all signs of prior problems appear to have vanished. His inner being somehow recentered itself, certainly without any kind of effective treatment from professionals, and he resumed his existence as teacher, philosopher, husband, and father. Indeed, my main memories of the time are of him as patient and gentle, as his response to my query about China and Russia clearly reveals.

He was promoted to associate professor at Ohio State early in the decade, receiving tenure based on his stellar work since graduate school days. But the repeated cycles were beginning to take a toll, even during the stable periods between episodes. Initially barely perceptible, the deficits showed up in subtle problems with organizing complex philosophical material in his scholarly writing. In addition, he had more difficulty motivating himself and showing sufficient concentration for original scholarship. His legendary sharpness began to wane, ever so slightly at first.

Compounding matters were the treatments he was beginning to receive. During several of his hospitalizations in the 1950s, he had regimens of ECT. In those days, many of the features that today make ECT a safe and effective intervention for treatment-resistant depressions were not present – for example, shorter duration of electric pulse and provision of full anesthesia to prevent injury during the induction of the seizure from the electric current. It is impossible to say how much of an effect the repeated ECTs had on his memory loss or cognitive slowing.[2]

For my father, the experience of receiving electroshock therapy was frightening. During one of our conversations many years later, he recalled the moments before a particular session. Several physicians, including the doctor who had become my father's outpatient psychiatrist, were attending at the hospital, preparing for the ECT. One of the doctors heard my father, who was on the table and about to be anesthetized, muttering subvocally. "What's he doing?" the doctor gruffly asked the others. "What do you think he's doing? He's praying!" retorted my father's own psychiatrist, realizing that my father had quietly begun reciting the Lord's Prayer in preparation for the treatment.

Back at home, following a hospitalization that included a number of ECT sessions, my mother watched with alarm and sadness as Virgil stood by the living room window, trying to recall the names of the neighbors. She stood next to him, coaching him on houses and names. He seemed dazed, confused. It was such incidents, my mother told me when I was well into adulthood, that made her realize that she would have to protect him during much of his subsequent life. Although his memory for the names of the neighbors soon returned, his organizational abilities and motivation for topflight philosophical scholarship never quite returned to their prior levels.

During this decade, specific medications were, for the first time in history, being developed and marketed to treat psychotic disorders. Indeed, because of his brother Bob's intervention, my father began to receive Thorazine in 1954 or 1955. He was, in fact, one of the earliest American patients to be prescribed this newly discovered medication, the first of the antipsychotic agents to be marketed. These medications are typically used in the treatment of schizophrenia, the diagnosis that my father had received. For the next two decades, he had regular prescriptions of Thorazine and, later, Mellaril (thioridizine), which he took at low, maintenance dosages during interepisode intervals and far higher dosages during his active episodes. Unfortunately, such "first-generation" antipsychotic medications produce more sedation than do many of the newer medications used to treat schizophrenia and other psychoses. And, as I discuss later, had he been accurately diagnosed with bipolar disorder and had specific treatments for this condition (such as lithium) been available in the United States at the time, his need for antipsychotic medications would undoubtedly have been reduced or even eliminated.

Because of the sleep disruption incurred by his episodes, his psychiatrist also began to prescribe barbiturates and other sleeping medications such as Doriden (glutethimide) for many years – indeed, for the remainder of his life. Fortunately, my father used these sleep medications only as prescribed and only at bedtime, never becoming addicted. Because of the poor quality of the medication-induced sleep that he received at night, he began a regular habit of taking an afternoon nap in the 1950s, which continued throughout his life. He probably received much of his untainted rapid-eye-movement (REM) sleep during these naps.

He was always extremely adherent to medication regimens, taking religiously whatever was prescribed. On several occasions he was also prescribed Dexedrine (dextroamphetamine), presumably to help lift him up from protracted low-energy, depressive states. He recalled later the euphoria induced by this stimulant, but he never took it for more than several weeks, as prescribed. I note also that although he enjoyed cocktails throughout his adult life, he never drank to excess, thereby escaping the fate of far too many individuals with severe mood disorders.[3]

My mother recalls that, at one point during the 1950s, my father's most beloved colleague, the longtime chairman of the philosophy department and a father figure to Virgil, called him in for a lengthy meeting to discuss his poor judgment with students. Inappropriate questions in class and during office hours, strange digressions from course material, inconsistencies in his approach to other people – all had been increasingly salient during the beginning stages of his episodes. In all likelihood, only academic tenure, which had accompanied his promotion to associate professor, had saved his job at such times.

On several occasions my mother had needed to contact my father's colleagues in order to discuss his growing irrationality and to make plans for enlisting medical help and even hospitalization. If my father surmised that she had made such phone calls, he would become even more upset, his paranoia now fueled. Partners and spouses must often walk on eggshells around a growing episode, planning in delicate, surreptitious ways in order not to engender rage or retaliation.

The recurrent episodes, the resultant chaos, the anger expressed toward my mother as his paranoia escalated, the retrenchment into lack of communication about the episodes or their aftermath, and, most importantly, the uncertainty as to when the next episode would ensue all began to take a toll on my mother. At one point during the late 1950s, she began to think seriously about the irrational and out-of-control behavior, the absences, and the lack of any assurance that the pattern would ever change. In what she later considered to be an extremely bold, even desperate move, she went to see a lawyer, raising the possibility that she might need to seek a divorce. Yet even within these confidential negotiations, she later told me, she could not bring herself to reveal the full nature of my father's behavior patterns and hospitalizations. As she put it, no one at that time really talked about mental illness in open ways.

Despite her advanced education, she had not worked outside the home since her marriage. Now, however, she had to consider such issues as custody and employment. She hoped beyond hope, however, that she would not need to pursue such a radical step as divorce.

The '50s: An Uphill Battle

What of my own recollections from this decade? One of my first memories was when I was three years old. I went one morning to the front door of our house, opened the door and retrieved the newspaper from the front step, and somehow made sense out of the letters of the headline and read the words to my parents. I remember most vividly the brightness of the sun and the excited feeling I had inside when the letters made the sound of words when I read them. I remember, too, the smiles of my mother and father.

A hazier memory from around that time is of going into my father's study in the basement and grabbing a book off the shelf, his favorite old dictionary that he had used since college days, leather bound. I must have liked the feel of the thin, onionskin pages and the gold embossing at their edge. I ripped some pages out of the book, not realizing that this was wrong but rather relishing the feel of the paper. My father later told me that although he was aghast that his prized dictionary was being dismantled, he never punished me but only took the book from my hands, teaching me to turn the pages. He did not want, he said, ever to discourage my interest in reading.

In fact, I can recall only one or two spankings that I ever received, each from my father after some transgression against my sister or some open defiance. Even then, I distinctly remember that my father was quite reluctant to give me as many as one or two swats on my clothed rear end; his punishment seemed reluctant. It is clear to me now that he didn't wish to continue the kinds of punishments he had received from his stepmother.

When I was in preschool and a bit older, my sister and I would sit in his lap after dinner, at the kitchen table of our first house, as he told us stories of Nickershoe, the Indian boy, repeating and embellishing stories that he had heard as a boy. I was enthralled. Sometimes I would wear a feather on a handmade headdress, probably fantasizing that I was the Indian boy. I also recall warm summer days on our front yard, following my father as he cut the grass with his power mover. I would lag several steps behind, pretending to be pushing my own mower. I loved to watch him shave, each morning, with his old straight razor in the bathroom. A few years later, he switched to an electric razor, carefully preparing his face before his careful shave, as I continued to watch intently.

One warm evening, when I was perhaps five or six, I came in from playing in the backyard. My mother was alone in the kitchen; perhaps my father was upstairs or in the study. I recall that it was still light outside, although evening was beginning to fall. I told her that I didn't want to be a child much longer, that I wanted to be older, to be grown up. Although her tone was laden with warmth and playfulness, I was a bit puzzled by her response: "Oh, Stevie, how you'll wish one day that you were still young. You'll have a lot of cares once you're older, a lot of responsibilities . . . How you'll wish you had been able to stay young." Only much later did I have any idea why she might have wished to protect me from the tribulations of growing older. It was about this time that she had begun to consult with the lawyer about the possibility of separation or divorce, though I knew nothing of these poignant and secretive negotiations.

My father passed the football with me during spare moments. He also worked with me on my baseball swing. He told me of his days as a shotputter, as well as his playing football in high school and junior college. I remember, as well, the days that he would take my sister and me to his office at the university. We would climb on the old fire escape at the back of the building, thrilled to have such a chance to play, and later smell the lingering pipe smoke in his book-lined office.

I realized only far later, of course, that he had needed on several occasions to return to this office – and his to teaching, advising, and writing – after having been hospitalized. He told me, during the talks we had once I became an adult, of paranoid encounters with colleagues during his escalating episodes, recounting the rage and irrationality he felt at the time. In how many faculty meetings or classes did he lose control? How many faculty, staff, and students wondered in amazement and confusion at his increasingly bizarre behaviors? On how many occasions did he have to pick up the pieces and continue, following an absence or a hospital stay, all the while wondering to himself who might be recalling and judging the behavior patterns that had led to his absence?

Again, throughout my childhood I was not aware that my father had any kind of mental illness. I knew only that he sometimes would be gone from the house, without any explanation, for shorter or longer periods of time. I knew also that no one talked about these absences or about the occasionally unusual behavior he exhibited when he was present. When he returned, nothing was said, and I somehow knew not to ask. Life just continued as before. I'm still not sure how my parents maintained such an extremely high level of control during his episodes as well as their deafening silence about his absences upon his return. Perhaps, at some level, they believed that if the events weren't talked about, they might just vanish from memory.

This stance of silence was reinforced by professional advice: "Do not tell your children about your condition," doctors told my father, "because they cannot comprehend mental illness." This silence, this guessing at what lay behind the absences, this containing of curiosity, this control over emotions – all in bipolar opposition to the intense, irrational behavior patterns that permeated the episodes themselves – are legacies of my childhood.

School was a refuge for me. I did well each year in my classes and liked to read, study, and do math. My parents were clearly proud of my schoolwork but conveyed their pride in an under-stated, satisfied manner. During "back to school" nights, when my parents attended classroom meetings with my teachers, my father would write warm, encouraging notes that appeared in my desk the next day.

Throughout childhood, I was close to my sister, Sally, fifteen months younger than I, and we continue to be emotionally close to this day. She was the bolder, braver one. When I was nearly four and she was not yet three years of age, we began a part-time program at the church preschool. I was terrified, not wanting to go, tearful and afraid once my mother was about to leave. "It's all right, big brother," my sister would say, consoling me and urging me to play with the other children. I followed her lead and, slowly, entered the group of teachers and other children.

As an adult, however, Sally has told me that she does not have the same kinds of warm childhood memories of my father as I do. I am not sure that he knew how to be as close or intimate with females as with males. His trust may well have eroded early on, related to the repeated punishments he received from his stepmother. I consider also that he had lost his mother at the age of three and that he had no sisters with whom he could relate.

The decade of the '50s was almost finished. My mother was on pins and needles, awaiting the next episode and wonder-ing whether her consultation with the lawyer would need to be pursued further. My sister and I literally slept through the worst of the turmoil at home, as was the case during my par-ents' drive to Cincinnati. Yet we were now beginning to enter a wider world of preschool and school, as my parents continued to face the daily challenges of home and work without any real communication about the crucial events of the decade. Where would it all lead?

The '50s: An Uphill Battle

In how many other families during this era did mental illness exist in silence? How many individuals had to learn, by trial and error, to cope with the unpredictability, the occasional terror, and the frequent despair? How many jobs were lost because of uncontrolled behavior? How many children coped alone, worried, wondering, and tending to blame themselves? I ask these questions rhetorically, for the answer must be enormous in terms of sheer numbers.

Despite the considerable progress of the last fifty years, these same questions could well be asked today. As highlighted in the recent report of the Surgeon General, mental disorders are still undetected, still vastly untreated even if detected, and still castigated and stigmatized.[4] Although there are signs of real hope, progress has been agonizingly slow.

At this point in the narrative, however, I am in elementary school, with my father's longest episode yet to emerge.

6

The '60s:
Vanished and
Returned

It is the spring of 1961, baseball season. I am eight years old, in the third grade, in my first year of Cub Scout baseball. It is a May evening, the light lingering until well past 8 p.m. Our team is playing in a league game.

My father has not been home, however, since the past September, when the school year began. Just vanished, no trace. When I ask where he is, my mother tells me, vaguely, that he is sick and that he is getting better in California. No phone calls or letters come from him. One day, my third-grade teacher asks about him, and I repeat what I have heard, that he's sick and in California. I remember her puzzled, doubtful expression that showed through her smile.

I try to keep busy with schoolwork and sports. After a few weeks, I don't really wonder about my dad all that often. I want to believe my mother, who assures me that he needs this rest. I continue to do well in school, feeling particularly excited on the days that tests are returned, looking forward to the good marks that I usually get. I have friends, though I don't talk with them about my dad.

My mother asks her brother, my uncle, to take me to some basketball games and to do some activities around Columbus. I am glad for these kinds of opportunities.

The '60s: Vanished and Returned

With spring's arrival, many of the boys are playing baseball. Although I am a decent athlete, I am thin and not all that confident, and I have never tried organized baseball before. My friends are joining the Cub Scout league, so I enroll, too, thanks to my mom's help.

But the season is difficult. For one thing, the other kids always seem to have their dads with them at practice and at games. Also, the Cub Scout league is for third, fourth, and fifth graders, so that the third graders, like me, are the smallest boys and worst players. Yet the rules state that every participant must play at least two innings in every game. The third graders usually get put in right field, during the middle innings, with the coaches hoping that no balls get hit their way, that they don't leave too many runners on base when they come to bat, and that these innings pass by uneventfully.

I am lonely during the games, sitting on the bench, wanting to see some action but dreading it, too. My confidence is low, and the coaches seem to spend their time with the older players during practice. I'm not only lonely but a little bit lost. I'm actually a bit afraid of the ball when the pitchers throw it fast or when it is hit hard to me when I'm in the field.

In this particular game, the coach looks down his roster and realizes that I haven't yet played. So off I go, into the lineup. As expected, I get placed in right field, the position least likely to involve any contact with the ball.

The sun is by now getting lower in the sky. Several players on the other team get hits or walks; two runners are now on base. I stand in right field, knowing that the other team is rallying and hoping that the ball won't get hit my way. As luck would have it, however, a left-handed batter comes up to the plate. Our pitcher throws it in and, CRRACK, the batter smashes a ball over the second baseman's head, hard into right field, bouncing in front of me.

I run to retrieve it. Running has never been a problem for me, as I'm fairly fast. But as soon as I reach the ball and pick it up, a strange thing happens: I freeze. My arm is cocked, but the ball seems to be stuck in my hand. I'm not sure whether or where to throw it.

It is like a dream. Time has slowed down. I sense the events around me, but I hold my pose with the ball in my hand, like a statue. I smell the grass and sense the late evening sky. I see the two runners circling the bases with the crowd cheering. I hear my coaches screaming, "Come on!" But still, I don't move. I know I should do something, but here I am, stuck. The diamond looks as though I'm seeing it through the wrong end of a telescope. The runners have now scored.

As I finally run in with the ball and toss it to an infielder from a short distance, my face is red. I see the coaches shaking their heads, the rest of the team baffled. I feel humiliated, knowing I've let them down. Part of me also wonders why someone hadn't shown me what to do earlier. But most of all I remember that frozen feeling, watching the runners circle the bases while I grow even more immobilized, with time seeming to stand still.

There's no one to talk with about it, after the game, so I just think about it, feeling lonelier, and finally go to sleep later that evening. I don't even wonder where my dad is.

My father went through a period without episodes at the end of the 1950s, leading my mother to suspend her thoughts of separation. In fact, life began to stabilize somewhat for the family. My parents decided to have a new home built several miles from the original family house, in a new subdivision of our suburban community. As the house was being completed, in the spring of 1960, my father was promoted to full professor, largely on the basis of his past record and his continuing (though at times interrupted) service and teaching.

In the late spring and early summer, my parents would drive Sally and me several miles north from our home to the site of the new house, at the edge of the suburb, on the border of miles of open land. A makeshift carnival had been set up in the parking lot of the new shopping center nearby. We begged our parents to take us there after we viewed the frame of the house, and we rode the rides and ate cotton candy, thrilled. That summer, between my second and third grade school years, the house was finally completed and we moved in. I was upset with having to leave my current elementary school, to which I had become loyal. But once we had settled in to the new house, I soon dropped my opposition to the move.

By the end of the summer, however, my father entered a protracted episode. It was severe enough that his brother Bob flew out once again from California to provide some stability and additional psychiatric consultation. After discussions with local professionals, it was decided that Virgil needed to be hospitalized in Los Angeles, in closer proximity to his brother. He was away for that entire school year, housed chiefly in a private psychiatric "lodge" and then spending some recovery time in his brother's home. Again, I was told only, and in the vaguest terms, that he was ill and that he needed to stay in California for some time.

From my mother's perspective, he might never have returned. During the fall of that school year she decided to reenter Ohio State to obtain a teaching credential, in order to be able to pursue regular employment. She realized that she might soon be thrust into the role of breadwinner. She had little communication from California, except for occasional updates from her brother-in-law.

Among my father's papers, I found a note he wrote in longhand, many years after this hospitalization, which recalled the beginnings of the episode and the journey to California. Note his "ideas of reference," in which he attaches special meanings to such everyday events as conversations among the passengers on the airplane:

The old "seance" insights – cf. flying to LA in 1960, 2nd leg: Thoughts about flying over my place of birth (outside Chicago) "reflected" in joint speech by several passengers.

This passage crowds the pages of a legal pad, with commentaries in the margins dizzyingly connected by arrows to the text. It was written in the 1980s, during what must have been a hypomanic episode, when he recalled this earlier period of elation and disorganization. It continues:

> In madness and high enthusiasm, bizarre behavior is explained by presence in the world of a mysterious power, which may enter the person and make him/her its instrument. In the Old Testament, power called *ruah* [*sic*] or *breath*. Thus Sampson's strength, the insanity of Saul.... An age was anticipated when God would "pour out his spirit on all flesh."... Cf. applications to feels, grimaces, gestures, etc., that "recall," however subtly, some previous gesture in a similar situation: A hand to wipe away a tear now when there is no tear.... an apparently warm buttocks when now thinking of or contemplating doing something for which act, when done as a youth or child, was thoroughly punished.

As always, remembrance of his childhood punishments permeated his memories and associations.

On another leaf of the pad, undated but undoubtedly written some time later, during a period of numb depression, are three small, cramped words, placed near the bottom of an otherwise blank page:

> So utterly bored

Bipolarities play themselves out even on the written page.

Back to my third grade year: I recall an event that took place during the long winter months. I wanted my mother to buy me a 45 r.p.m. record of a popular song that was being played on the radio. She soon bought it for me. When I eagerly played it on the turntable, it skipped repeatedly, obviously flawed. With utter frustration, I said, "Oh, God." I recall my mother's stern disappointment that I had used this language, as well as my own guilt over having done so. In fact, my maternal grandmother, who lived in Columbus and who was quite religious, was at this time giving my sister and me moral lessons on those evenings that we would spend the night at her home. Although these were nights full of adventure and fun at her stately, old, wood-floored home on the other side of town, I internalized her words and began looking in the Bible to find passages stating that taking the Lord's name in vain would lead to everlasting damnation. My guilt and fear were fueled even further.

My mother was strong, and she was always present for me during my childhood. I realize now, however, that it was difficult for her to let me or my sister express many of the frustrations or fears we might have had, as she herself worked to maintain control, actively contemplating that her husband might never return. Indeed, this was the husband whose irrational behavior, paranoia, and verbal outbursts were often directed toward her. Maintaining control was her only choice. Who, in fact, supported her? Certainly not my father's doctors, who excluded her from any treatment efforts, probably under the misguided edict of confidentiality and the stance that all therapy must be individual in nature (as opposed to including the family). And not her own mother, who wouldn't have fully understood or accepted conceptions of mental illness. And certainly not my father himself, who had returned from prior episodes and hospitalizations remarkably improved but silent about his experiences and his terror. Such silence is, unfortunately, contagious.

During this year I also began to develop fears of not being able to fall asleep at night. I would worry terribly about bad words or thoughts that would pop into my head at bedtime, fueling my fear that I would never get to sleep. I tried to suppress the profane expressions from coming into my mind, by counting or saying certain calming words and phrases. I also began to believe that I needed to urinate, beginning a nightly cycle of repeated trips to the bathroom. Once I had gone to bed, I would worry that I might still have to "go," constantly returning to the toilet, to make sure that I was fully ready to get to sleep. It seems that my religious fears, spurred through my own reading of certain Bible passages, had convinced me that I would suffer forever unless I were quite controlled in my behavior.

My mother was sufficiently concerned about the apparent problem with urination that she set up an appointment at a hospital for me to have X-rays taken. I recall going to the hospital and putting on the funny gown that tied at the back. Later, I heard that no physical problems had been noted. I wasn't really surprised, as I had suspected as much myself. I now interpret some of these nighttime fears and rituals as related to a kind of separation anxiety: My father had disappeared, but I didn't really know how or why. I felt that I needed to maintain rigid control over my behavior, probably as a means of ensuring that I was virtuous (and perhaps aiding my father's return in some way). I must have been guarding against the fears and assuring my "goodness" by praying to myself or saying numbers in rigorous order, in what amounted to a kind of obsessional way of coping. These clinical terms, however – separation anxiety, obsessional rituals – seem lifeless, unable to do justice to the loneliness and fright that I felt.

It was during the spring that I played my initial year of baseball and had my experience in right field, which only furthered my loneliness. Schoolwork, however, continued to be a refuge, along with a sense inside myself that I would make it through all of this. I didn't deliver any kinds of pep talks to myself or display false bravado. Rather, I just seemed to believe that I'd be okay, maybe even special, especially in schoolwork.

The '60s: Vanished and Returned

My fears and rituals diminished somewhat after my father returned, an entire school year later. Nothing special was said about his homecoming; indeed, I cannot even recall the day he came back in the summer. Instead, life gradually returned to how it had been before.

I entered fourth grade. As my mother was now taking university courses, my father cooked breakfast each day. He would then hurry off to the university for his day's teaching and meetings. I had a gifted fourth-grade teacher at my public school, and learned a tremendous amount about history, geography, and even the Bible. Indeed, this teacher emphasized lessons from the New Testament throughout her instruction. As one extra credit lesson, I memorized all sixty-six books of the Bible. I certainly thought about right and wrong each day, and I continued to carry my worries about morality and even mortality to bed at night.

One night during this fourth-grade year I awakened, quite frightened, in the middle of the night. I had undoubtedly fallen asleep for a period of several hours but, as would often happen, once I woke up I believed that I hadn't fallen asleep at all and that I was destined to lie awake all night. Crying hard, and nearly panic-stricken, I knocked at my parents' bedroom door.

My father came out and patiently walked me back to my bedroom. He started to soothe me to sleep as I lay in my bed. He sensed that I was really upset. I told him, through my tears, that I was afraid that I might die soon. He immediately responded, quietly but with conviction. "Son, you live in an age of miracles. Doctors are able to treat many diseases with new medicines. When I was growing up, there weren't the antibiotics and other medicines that have now been discovered. Just think of what new discoveries will come in the future. Why, you'll probably live to be 100 years old!" Although I was still upset, his words began to calm me. This magical number of 100, as with the kindergarten vignette of the populations of

73

Russia and China, helped me to return peacefully to sleep. My father knew how to settle me, even though he must have had plenty inside himself to settle after his year away. How much was he wondering about his next episode, and when it might take over? How aware was he that he was beginning to lose his edge cognitively and professionally, for reasons beyond his control? To what extent was he wondering whether some of the new medicines to which he referred might help him with his periodic bouts of madness? Whatever his own thoughts, he was able to calm me in a time of real need.

Around this time, I recall seeing my father patiently sit with my mother at the kitchen table or our picnic table outside to assist her with her more difficult coursework in logic and transformational grammar. She had drawn the attention of the chair of the English Department at Ohio State, who asked her, following completion of a second Master's in English, to teach university English rather than take up secondary school teaching. She decided to do so and began a fifteen-year period of teaching English to foreign students and the required freshman English course at Ohio State.

Also during the 1960s, our family took several plane trips to California to visit my father's relatives. The first trip was over Easter vacation in 1964, when I was eleven. The trip began with difficulty, as my father, in his haste to pack up the family car en route to the airport, closed the door on his thumb, nearly breaking it. Ever stoic, he did not hesitate to get us to the airport on time. In Pasadena, I met my father's stepmother at his boyhood home, where she still lived. She seemed grandmotherly enough to me, and I recall her commenting on what a festive occasion it was to have so many of the family members together.

One of my uncles, Randall, the economist, looked over my sixth-grade autobiography that I had brought along, which was entitled "My Life, By Me." I remember that in the

74

introduction to this rather lengthy work I had written a statement about the lucky, fortunate life I led, a statement that I wholeheartedly believed. I recall Randall's commenting to my father: "...he's philosophical, just like you."

During this visit, we drove to a department store near Pasadena called "Hinshaw's," named for a relative of my father's who had founded the small chain. I couldn't believe that the family name was in such big letters on the sign over the store. We went to a back office, where I met the founder, a man in his sixties. He was in a wheelchair, however, and I remember that he could not speak clearly and that he drooled. He seemed, in fact, quite disconnected. I had been told that he was the owner of the store and also that he had a disease called Parkinson's.

Less than two years later, on another trip, we returned to the store. To my surprise, he was smiling, walking, and talking as we went to greet him, appearing nearly normal. I couldn't believe that it was the same person. My father explained to me afterward, gently but intensely, that a new medication, called L-DOPA, had helped to treat his cousin's disease. I was amazed that a medication could have such a dramatic effect on a person's functioning, and I wondered how a pill could affect the brain and muscles in such a striking way.* Since that visit, I have thought more than once that my father must have been actively wondering whether a similar type of medicine might one day help his own mental state.

---

* L-DOPA does help to alleviate symptoms of Parkinson's disease, but for individuals with "complex" Parkinson's (i.e., with dementia as well) it is not nearly as helpful. Even for uncomplicated Parkinson's, its early status as a miracle drug has been downgraded on the basis of accumulating evidence. Indeed, response is far from complete in most cases, and benefits are not typically long-term in nature. Initial studies with highly selected patients under carefully controlled circumstances yielded higher estimates of its benefits than did subsequent trials with complex cases in real-world circumstances. The same is true for medications like lithium for bipolar disorder.

For much of the 1960s, my father was euthymic, without major episodes. He did sometimes experience periods of flat depression that would persist for some months, but he did not cycle into expansive, destructive manias.

During the summer of 1964 my parents, maternal grandmother, sister, and I drove to New York for a trip the World's Fair. One evening, following a subway ride to Queens for a day spent visiting all of the exhibits, a call came through to the hotel room back in Manhattan. My father looked upset, and he spoke slowly after the call, saying that Grandma Hinshaw (his stepmother) had died that day. He decided that he must fly back to California for the funeral. For a time I was despondent, thinking that the vacation would come to an end. To my relief, my mother and grandmother decided to continue the vacation with my sister and me, driving us through New England as my father was in Pasadena for the funeral. When he returned, he looked a bit sad, but he did not develop an episode.

Although I did not know it at the time, my father's career had clearly reached its peak. He continued to teach actively, but scholarly publications were sparse or absent for many years. He taught esoteric graduate seminars in philosophy of science as well as introductory undergraduate philosophy. Indeed, he always loved teaching the "intro" course, with Descartes on the top of his list of favorite philosophers. He was impressed with Descartes's having challenged all belief, returning to first principles to rebuild a philosophy and a vision of the world and of God. Increasingly, my father viewed philosophy as a way of connecting his spiritual interests with the complexities of modern science. "How many quintillions of atoms are there in a handful of air?" he would ask rhetorically both when I was young and again when I was an adult. "If we look at the real nature of the world, it is full of miracles." I believe that he saw philosophy as a means of confronting the ineffable mysteries of life and existence. He was deeply spiritual, and philosophy was, for him, a means of bridging religion and science.

Politically, he was quite liberal, putting him at odds with much of the local population in Columbus and even many of the faculty at Ohio State. He had a vision of universities as settings in which free thought and speech should always be encouraged.

In the early '60s, not long after his return from the lengthy California hospitalization, he began singing in the choir of the Protestant church that our family attended, rehearsing each Thursday night and singing two services each Sunday. He had always loved choral, religious music. The choir was first-rate; the new music director was a passionate organist and conductor. The music was a key part of my father's spiritual life.

One day in the middle of the 1960s, when I was in junior high school, my father took a long phone call from California, originating from his brother Bob. He got off the phone shaken, explaining that, because of the sedentary nature of my uncle's work as a psychiatrist, he had lost circulation in a leg, which had needed to be amputated. I thought that the explanation wasn't quite adequate at the time, but it wasn't until some years later that I came to realize that self-administered injections of painkillers, taken initially for migraines, were the real culprit. During the next family visit to California, we saw my uncle – jovial, intellectual, and witty – walking from his Cadillac convertible with a limp that betrayed his artificial leg.

My father continued to be tuned in to my emotions. In 1967, I entered tenth grade, moving up from junior high to high school. I had a critical decision to make: whether to play football for our high school's highly successful team or to run cross-country, a sport at which I thought I probably could do better but which was a far lonelier endeavor. I had played organized football for the first time only the year before, in ninth grade on the junior high school team, an activity that my father had supported, given his early experiences in the sport. I was still thin, however, and wondered whether I could really make it at the high-school level. Our teams were known around the state as strong, so the competition even to make the team was fierce. During the late summer, I decided to join the cross-country team instead of starting twice-daily football practices in August.

Within a week, however, I was miserable, escalating quickly to inconsolable. I could see the football team practice at the high-school field, through our backyard, and I felt that I had ruined my only opportunity to prove myself in this way. I also felt that for the next three years, I would be missing out on being with the group of guys I really wanted to join. I believed that I had left behind a key opportunity irrevocably, and I despaired in consequence. The sense of loneliness and of having missed out permanently on a key opportunity was overwhelming.

Not knowing what to do, and feeling that all was lost, I tearfully told my father about my feelings. He listened patiently and said that he would get in touch with the coach, a tough but fair and honorable man. I hoped beyond hope that something could be worked out; at least, I now had an option, some active means of coping. Later that day, my father said that he had in fact reached the coach by phone and that he would drive me over to the coach's house that evening. There, I could explain the situation and see whether it wasn't too late to start practice. I waited in the living room while my dad spoke with the coach first, then entered the dining room to speak with him alone. I spoke as bravely as I could. With my father's having laid the groundwork, the coach allowed me to join the practices.

I then played for the junior varsity along with the other tenth graders. I certainly didn't star, but I was doing what I wanted to do and showed some talent. I continued playing for the varsity during my eleventh grade year, relishing our Friday night games, under the lights, in front of thousands of fans. I don't think that I ever really thanked my father enough for intervening in just the right way on my behalf. He had known just when and how to intervene, and it was a turning point in my high school life.

By twelfth grade I was starting for the varsity, although I was just an average player on a fine team. We had been the undefeated state champions of Ohio for two years running, and each game we played was a chance to extend our winning streak. My sister Sally was a sophomore in high school, intent on becoming a cheerleader. I was so immersed in the season and our own undefeated team, as well as with applying to college, and she was so immersed in her activities, that we hardly noticed my father's growing irrationality during the fall. I do remember, in October, that I dropped a touchdown pass in a game (which we were winning handily) and later came home full of self-hatred, tears, and self-recrimination. My father tried to reach out and console me, clearly upset by my distress, wondering how he could take away my pain. I could see the pain in his own eyes as he groped for the right thing to say and do.

Later that fall, he received day hospitalization at the university's psychiatric service, but my own denial and my parents' superhuman efforts at hiding the situation from Sally and me kept me from becoming aware of the extent of his disturbance. He weathered the episode, with increased dosages of antipsychotic medication, without the full decompensation of most of his previous bouts.

How could I fail to notice my father's emerging disorganization during the fall of my senior year of high school? Being immersed in a battle for the state football championship was certainly a distraction, as was applying to college and having a steady girlfriend. I was busy, and I was spending less time at home. But I also believe that I didn't really want to see what

79

was in front of my eyes. My mother and father were also still working hard to suppress his symptoms and keep the worst of it from my sister and me. Silence, denial, and control continued, and I had now internalized them.

Our team ended up undefeated, with the number-one ranking in the state. I then switched to the basketball team, but concentrated more than ever on my studies.

Regarding college, I had applied to several small schools in Ohio but had also given a shot at a number of Ivy League schools. In the spring, I learned that I had been accepted at each school to which I had applied. Having already driven back east to visit these colleges a month earlier, I selected Harvard, largely because of its prestige and also because I realized that I wanted to be in a new area of the country.

In June, I spoke at my high school graduation as class valedictorian, to a full gymnasium huddled indoors because of thunderstorms. I then worked at summer jobs and kept in shape by running and weightlifting. I began to read as much psychology as I could find. The study of the mind had, rather suddenly, motivated me as no other subject matter had throughout high school. Although we had no courses in psychology at our high school, I began to read Freud as well as several other books in my father's home library. Things were starting to shift; I was beginning to find an intellectual direction that sparked my interest. With a few weeks, I knew, I would be starting a new life at college.

7

Diagnosis and Misdiagnosis

A key question at this point in the narrative, following the descriptions of a number of my father's episodes, is why he was continuing to be diagnosed with the disorder called schizophrenia. He had received this diagnosis from mid-adolescence until he was over fifty years of age, even though his episodes were defined by a clearly cyclic course and a regaining of "normal" or near-normal levels of functioning in between. Weren't such features known to be clear indicators of bipolar disorder? To address this mystery, in this chapter I describe bipolar disorder in more detail and then discuss the history of diagnostic thinking in psychiatry that permeated America during the twentieth century. This discussion is not an attempt at a complete description of the disorder; for this purpose, I recommend several scholarly and more popular books.[1]

Features of Bipolar Disorder

When my father entered a manic episode, he developed nearly the full complement of symptoms that characterize this condition. During the initial weeks, as noted in Chapter 5, he showed classic signs of the first stage of mania, also called hypomania: hyperacusis (his perceptions of colors, sounds, tastes, and textures were enhanced and laden with sensuousness); decreased need for sleep; preoccupation with expansive, grand ideas and sexual themes and images; feelings of religious ecstasy (drawing on his life history of religious training); rapid speech and behavior; wordplay and puns. That particular sparkle, or gleam, in his eye would emerge, signifying his religious preoccupation or his absorption with grand, philosophical ideas and prompting a sense of impending terror to my mother, who knew that uncontrolled and extremely irrational behavior might soon follow.

Initially, many of these symptoms of hypomania could be quite compelling to others. He was full of ideas, quick with his wit, and laden with energy. Yet as his talkativeness and charm progressed into utter self-absorption, he would become overbearing rather than sociable. Indeed, during his progression through hypomania, his judgment would become clouded and his interpersonal boundaries blurred.

Some individuals with bipolar disorder do not "advance" beyond this set of symptoms to more severe phases of mania. Through mechanisms that are not well understood, the symptoms peak at this stage, even without treatment. Such patients are diagnosed with what is termed "bipolar II" disorder, referring to a history of hypomanic episodes, usually interspersed with periods of depression. It might seem, at first glance, that this variant would be fairly benign clinically, or even quite desirable, given the surge of energy and productivity that often emerge from hypomania. But, unfortunately, afflicted individuals often have depressions that can be quite severe. In fact, the suicide risk for persons with Bipolar II is high. Although the manic symptoms are somehow self-limiting, the disorder carries serious ramifications across the life course.

Several of my father's episodes peaked at this stage before slowly fading away of their own accord, although most of his episodes progressed to far more severe levels. There is considerable variability in the course of manic episodes, not only across people but also within the same person at different points in time.

This hypomanic "high" is quite similar, in many respects, to the rush that individuals may experience when taking strong stimulants like cocaine. Indeed, in both cases, surges of release of the neurotransmitter dopamine are clearly implicated. The euphoria in both instances can be quite addictive, leading many persons with bipolar disorder to crave their next episode, despite the consequences and devastation that accrue when the hypomanic symptoms advance to subsequent stages or when the other "pole" of the disorder, serious depression, wreaks its havoc. Not surprisingly, drug abuse can be a devastating accompaniment to bipolar disorder, as afflicted persons attempt to mimic their natural high through chemical means.

Typically, my father would advance from hypomania directly to the next stage of mania, termed stage 2, or full mania. Although there is actually no clear boundary between these stages, at some point, his perceptual world and his reasoning would begin to disintegrate. A clear sign would be when everyday events took on highly personalized meanings (e.g., the televised singer conveying special messages directly to him over the airwaves), also known as ideas of reference. At other times the "messages" might be conveyed to him by the patterns of speech from fellow passengers on an airplane. For other individuals, the signals might involve the changing of a traffic light or patterns made by windowshades – some drawn, some open – on a walk down a city street. How thrilling, at first, to realize that secret messages are being conveyed, only to you! Soon, however, the fascination gives way to terror, particularly if, as is often the case, the messages begin to convey malevolent or harmful intent.

Indeed, ideas of reference are often the first signs of an impending paranoia. The individual must now be extremely vigilant: What new signal might soon be delivered, conveying yet another message? Almost inevitably, increasing disorganization in thought and speech becomes evident. For my father, the initial quickening of thought and speech during hypomania would begin to exceed the "speed limit," portending reckless thinking processes and lack of judgment. Recall the midnight drive to Cincinnati, leaving the children at home, shattering the speed limits literally. Although disorganization is a word used to describe the behavioral patterns at this stage, the kinds of gross misjudgment, dramatic alteration of daily routine, and frenzied behavior patterns far surpass the usual meaning of the term "disorganized." Such features as wanton spending of money, in order to pursue a whim or fuel a scheme, and the damaging of relationships, through grandiose demands or sexual acting out, are often present. From this perspective, the puzzlement and even anger on the part of partners and fellow workers who aren't able to keep up with the increasingly frenetic and irrational "program" of the mania are all too understandable.

By this second stage of mania, the euphoria – that is, the giddy, expansive sense of wonder and energy that characterized the hypomanic phase – has given way to irritability, a sense of entitlement, and even rage. Irritable mood can permeate hypomania as well. In fact, the common belief that mania is invariably euphoric and pleasurable is mythical. Thus, diagnostic criteria for hypomania and mania now specify either a euphoric or an irritable mood.[2] By stage 2, the rest of the world has trouble keeping pace with the grand plans, the phone calls at all hours of the night, the discoveries of hidden meaning behind everyday events, and the building irritability and perturbation of the afflicted individual. Others' attempts to reason with or thwart the snowballing, frantic activity are often met with hostility. It is clear that by this point events have escalated to a critical level.

During this second stage of mania it is almost inevitable that the ideas of reference, poor judgment, breakdowns of perceptual experiences, incipient paranoia, and angry self-absorption coalesce into what is known as psychosis. Psychotic behavior includes several interrelated symptoms: severely disordered thinking; behavioral agitation; hallucinations, which are perceptual experiences without a real stimulus present (such as hearing voices); and delusions, which are unshakable, false, even bizarre beliefs. By the time that psychosis emerges, rational thought has broken down in fundamental ways, as the individual enters a world of distorted logic as well as utterly strange and often terrifying experiences.

At age sixteen, my father's sleepless, confused, agitated state in the late summer gave way to grossly illogical thinking, auditory hallucinations, and frank delusions. The latter were characterized vividly by his conviction that he had the ability to fly and that his jumping from the porch roof could send a message to stop Hitler. Soon thereafter, warehoused in the county hospital for nearly six months, he heard "celestial music of the spheres, all night long," evidence of auditory hallucinations. Additional delusional beliefs during his institutionalization had devastating consequences: Most saliently, he became convinced that his food was being poisoned and that he must therefore stop eating. This fixed, paranoid belief nearly cost him his life.

Eventually, my father's disorganization and chaotic thinking and behavior would become so severe that he had entered stage 3, or what is sometimes termed disorganized mania. At this point, the symptomatology is indistinguishable from that of severe cases of paranoid schizophrenia or so-called disorganized schizophrenia, in which devastatingly severe psychosis is coupled with an utter loss of behavioral and emotional control. By this point, work is no longer possible and home life has inevitably collapsed. Behavior may alternate between

85

wild agitation and stupor. Logical thought no longer occurs. Psychiatric hospitalization is inevitable during this third stage of mania, if it hasn't been required already.

The classic accounting of these stages is found in the work of Carlson and Goodwin, who documented the course of untreated patients with bipolar disorder through careful observation on a research hospital ward.[3] They noted that the lengths of time that different patients spent in each stage was quite variable and that stages are not always clearly demarcated from one another. Nonetheless, their observation that, beyond hypomania, manic episodes almost inevitably involved psychotic levels of functioning was groundbreaking.

In persons with bipolar disorder, manic cycles usually alternate, in varying ways, with episodes of depression. There is no universal pattern in this regard. Some afflicted individuals have an initial episode of mania, plunging immediately afterward into a devastating depression. Others show the reverse pattern, with a major depression appearing as the first episode. Episodes often begin during adolescence but may emerge later in life as well. In most individuals with bipolar disorder, there are periods of euthymic mood in between episodes. Sometimes, as in the case of my father, the period of normal functioning might last for months or even years. But for others, the cycling is far more rapid, with little time spent in a normal mood state before the next episode ensues. In fact, during so-called rapid cycling, manic and depressed cycles are extremely brief, with several episodes per year.[4] The tumultuousness of life for such persons is scarcely imaginable.

Once again, individual differences are the rule. In some instances, several depressive cycles may appear before a manic episode; in others, manic episodes may predominate prior to a depression. My father's depressions, in fact, were not composed of distinct, plunging episodes but rather as "flat," empty periods of days, weeks, or even months.

Diagnosis and Misdiagnosis

Diagnostically speaking, even one hypomanic or manic episode qualifies the individual for a diagnosis of bipolar disorder, bipolar I for instances of full mania, bipolar II for cases in which hypomania is the "highest" level of the manic symptomatology. In contrast, so-called unipolar depression constitutes recurrent episodes of depressions as the sole mood disturbance.

Because of the individuality of these patterns, clinicians must obtain a thorough history of each patient, which may help to assess the pattern of the person's cycles. Otherwise, there is no valid way to predict the course ahead of time. Even with such a history, prediction is usually still uncertain, meaning that patients must be quite vigilant with respect to the next episode that may emerge. It is also essential for the clinician to supplement data from the patient himself or herself with information from people who are close to the patient, such as family members, partners, or workmates. The reason is that personal insight is often poor in bipolar disorder, as distortions, denial, or simple lack of access to crucial information are all too commonplace. Indeed, breakdowns of judgment and of accurate self-reflection are part and parcel of the unfolding episodes. Thus, involving others in the assessment process is necessary, but this was a practice that was clearly not followed throughout much of my father's life.

Manic episodes usually last several weeks, although some are considerably longer. Depressions tend to last longer, averaging several months; but again, some are far more protracted. In fact, in what is termed dysthymic disorder, depressive mood states may linger for many months or even years at a stretch. Yet recall also that in persons with rapid cycling, episodes may alternate in periods of one or two days.

Several other features of bipolar disorder warrant mention. First, I reiterate that the common perception that manic states are always pleasurable and expansive is inaccurate. In a large number of cases the predominant affective state is one of irritability, which can escalate into frank anger. Second, even though manic cycles are nearly always time-limited (even in the absence of treatment), the severity and consequences of the symptoms often yield a terrible toll, especially in advanced stages of mania or depression. A devastating number of consequences can accrue from an episode of a few weeks' or months' duration.

Indeed, the economic impact of bipolar disorder is alarming: marked declines in productivity, the experience of job loss, and rampant personal and family devastation.[5] At the level of the afflicted individual, consequences of sexual acting out, bankruptcy, ruined relationships, cardiac arrest (from the exhaustion attending to nonstop activity), high risk for accidents, and substance abuse may well emanate from mania. In an extremely large proportion of cases, self-destructive impulses are likely to appear. The impulse control problems characteristic of mania, coupled with the morbid thoughts, exhaustion, and delusional thinking that often accompany severe bipolar disorder, comprise a lethal combination. Without treatment, in fact, the estimates of completed suicide for persons with bipolar disorder range as high as 20 percent, astronomically higher than the rate for the general population and higher, in fact, than that for unipolar depression or nearly any other psychiatric disorder.[6] Rates of attempted suicide are far higher.[7]

As might be expected, the suicidal thoughts and actions occur most often during the depressive poles of bipolar cycles. Yet they may appear at other times as well. Indeed, persons with bipolar disorder often experience mental states that blend the energy of mania with the despair and hopelessness of severe depression. As I noted earlier, these are termed "mixed states," which appear to be far more prevalent than the common depiction of pure manias alternating with pure depressions in the life course of individuals with bipolar disorder.[8] Indeed, much of stage 2 and stage 3 mania contains admixtures of manic-level energy with highly morbid, depressive, self-destructive impulses. When agitation, hopelessness, psychotic thought processes, impulsivity, and risk for substance abuse are added to the mix, the risk for suicidal thought and action rises precipitously.

Other issues regarding bipolar disorder are provocative. First, it is a disorder that is decidedly episodic and recurrent. A person who experiences one manic episode has a greater than 90 percent chance of experiencing subsequent manias and/or depressions.[9] Second, at least in the Northern Hemisphere, the peak occurrence of manic episodes is in the late summer to early fall, presumably as the proportion of daylight begins to taper, whereas depressions cluster in the spring, with April consistently appearing as the peak month for suicides. My father had a high percentage of his hypomanic or manic episodes that began in the summer and fall months. Intriguingly, there appears to be a reversal of these trends in the Southern Hemisphere.[10] Third, despite the overwhelming evidence for biological underpinnings of bipolar disorder – most notably, a huge genetic liability[11] – psychological factors (in particular, loss events or those stressors that disrupt daily sleep-wake cycles) are important for the onset and timing of episodes and even their recovery periods.[12] It is also becoming accepted that chronic stress, including the stress induced by substance use and abuse, is involved in precipitating episodes for individuals with underlying genetic vulnerability to bipolar disorder and that physical or sexual abuse may portend a particularly difficult course of bipolar disorder for those who have been victims.[13] Overall, the chain of events implicated in the risks for and manifestations of bipolar disorder is complex. I take up causal factors, including some of the specific triggers related to my father's episodes, in Chapter 11.

A Clash of Paradigms

Back to the issue at hand: Why was my father so persistently misdiagnosed for much of his life? Although it is now known that when manic episodes move beyond stage 1 they typically encompass the harrowing symptoms of psychosis, this view was not at all accepted for much of the last century. In fact, a fundamentally different idea of classification held sway.

For over fifty years, American psychiatry espoused the position of the Swiss psychiatrist Eugen Bleuler, who coined the term "schizophrenia" early in the twentieth century to classify together a variety of psychotic features and disorders that had been reported clinically for many years.[14] Bleuler contended that psychotic symptoms (chiefly, delusions and hallucinations) are actually secondary features of schizophrenia's basic pathologic process, which involves a splitting of the mind's cognitive functions from one another and from the emotions. In fact, the term schizophrenia is Greek for "split mind." (Note that this splitting does not imply the "split personalities" of multiple personality disorder, now termed dissociative identity disorder, which is a separate, controversial diagnostic category.) In Bleuler's conception, psychotic symptoms invariably and inevitably reflect this deeper, underlying schizophrenic process, even though this latter process is not directly visible to the observer or clinician. The psychotic symptoms are therefore the overt signal that an underlying schizophrenic disorder is occurring beneath the surface. The upshot, from this perspective, is that the presence of psychosis warrants a diagnosis of schizophrenia.

Bleuler's views took hold in the United States in much the same way that Freudian psychoanalytic perspectives became the mainstay of American psychological and psychiatric thinking. Like such psychodynamic ideas, which posited that overt behavior is rooted in unobservable, unconscious processes, the Bleulerian view held that observable psychosis signaled deep undercurrents. The diagnostic implication was clear: If any symptoms of psychosis were present, then an underlying schizophrenic process was lurking beneath the surface and the diagnosis of schizophrenia was mandatory.

The main contrasting view was embodied in Emil Kraepelin's conceptions of psychopathology. This German psychiatrist was not enamored of unobservable processes but instead concentrated on precise description of symptomatology throughout the lifespan. Subdividing the major adult disorders, he coined the term "dementia praecox" around the turn of the twentieth century, contrasting it with "maniacal depressive insanity," or what we today call bipolar disorder.[15] According to Kraepelin, dementia praecox is a relatively rare disorder, in which the onset of psychotic symptoms in adolescence or early adulthood ("praecox," akin to the English term "precocious") is followed by progressive cognitive deterioration (hence, "dementia"). In his view, dementia praecox is therefore one type of psychotic disorder, distinguishable from other forms of psychosis by its progressively deteriorating course across the lifespan.

From Kraepelin's perspective, dementia praecox could not be differentiated from manic-depressive disorder on the basis of psychotic symptoms per se, which may well occur in each disorder, but instead by its developmental course or natural history. In other words, whereas dementia praecox is marked by a progressive, inevitable decline in mental powers and overall psychological functioning – even as particular psychotic symptoms might wax and wane – in manic-depressive illness, the cycles (although featuring psychotic symptoms at their extreme phases) are interspersed with a return to normal functioning between episodes. If clinicians were to evaluate each disorder at its height of psychotic functioning, they could not distinguish them. Rather, the distinction must be made chiefly on the basis of the timing and patterning of episodes across development.

European psychiatry held to the Kraepelinian perspective throughout the last century. In contrast, because of the acceptance of Bleuler's views in the United States,[16] nearly any patient in America who, like my father, showed psychotic features during stage 2 or 3 of mania inevitably received a diagnosis of schizophrenia. In extremely rare cases, an individual might receive a diagnosis of manic-depressive illness in this country, but only if she or he did not show psychotic features during cycles, delimiting this diagnosis to relatively mild cases.

My father's symptoms during his initial episode of 1936 were clearly psychotic in nature: Auditory hallucinations, bizarre delusions, considerable agitation, and disordered thinking pervaded his clinical picture. At that point in American history, a diagnosis of schizophrenia was virtually inevitable. The return of psychotic features during his episodes of the 1940s, 1950s, and 1960s undoubtedly reaffirmed this diagnostic formulation, as the psychotic content of the symptoms rather than the episodic nature of the cycles constituted the key criterion for diagnosis.

The broad American conception of schizophrenia versus the narrow European view was strikingly documented in a study funded by the World Health Organization during the 1960s, in which the prevalence of mental disorders was ascertained in a number of nations. As diagnosed by clinicians from each home nation, schizophrenia was found to be eight times more frequent in New York than in London, a great difference in prevalence.[17] This differential rate disappeared, however, when an international team applied a consistent set of diagnostic criteria, revealing that it was the divergent diagnostic conceptions and practices rather than any true difference in prevalence that underlay the discrepancy. In other words, rates of schizophrenia and of bipolar disorder are remarkably consistent across cultures and nations when standardized diagnostic systems are utilized.

In the 1970s, American psychiatry moved from a psychodynamic focus to a more symptom-based conception of mental disorders. As such, it began to shift to a view more consistent with European and Kraepelinian perspectives, reserving the diagnosis of schizophrenia for severe and long-lasting psychoses that typically do not show pronounced interepisode recovery. With this perspective came the realization that bipolar disorder was more common than had been officially thought. The official diagnostic criteria did not shift formally until the beginning of the next decade, with the publication in 1980 of the third edition of the American Psychiatric Association's diagnostic guide, the *Diagnostic and Statistical Manual of Mental Disorders* (DSM-III).[18] In this version, as well as in more recent editions of this psychiatric "bible,"[19] it is explicitly recognized that bipolar disorder is frequently accompanied by psychotic features, even "mood-incongruent" delusions and hallucinations that are quite bizarre and apparently quite unrelated thematically to the predominant mood state.* The difference from past diagnostic thinking in American was striking.

In later life, as my father began to learn more about his condition, he told me that he believed his appropriate diagnosis was that of "unipolar mania," a rare variant of bipolar

---

* As diagnostic conceptions were beginning to shift in the United States, the contention was made that psychotic symptoms could indeed accompany depressions or manias (if the episodes were sufficiently severe), but that such symptoms would be "mood congruent." Thus, a manic delusion might be the belief that one had been placed on the earth as the new Messiah; a depressive hallucination might involve the individual's hearing voices that speak of her worthlessness. These types of psychotic symptoms were contrasted with the bizarre types of delusions and hallucinations believed to characterize schizophrenia (e.g., the belief that radio transmitters had been placed inside one's head). Today, however, the diagnostic criteria have shifted to the perspective that if a mania or depression reaches severe levels, even bizarre psychotic symptoms that are incongruent with the underlying mood may be present.

disorder in which manic episodes predominate, without the usual course of depressions that alternate with manias. (Note that such exclusive manias would still be diagnosed as bipolar disorder, as even one manic episode mandates this diagnosis.) His perceptions may have been correct to some extent, in that his major episodes were of the manic variety. I do not believe, however, that he was fully accurate. His lack of insight, common among patients with severe mental illness, prevented him from recognizing the minor and moderate depressions from which he periodically suffered in between his manic episodes, as well as the mixed states (once again, those admixtures of agitated behavior with dysphoric or despairing mood) into which his manias would typically devolve. It was the agitated, wild, out-of-control manias with their attendant paranoia and thought disorder that stayed in my father's memory as the personal legacy of his mental disturbance.

Current Diagnostic Thinking and Specific Treatments for Bipolar Disorder

Although the diagnostic standards regarding schizophrenia versus bipolar disorder have clearly changed in the United States over the last several decades, is the switch to a European perspective correct? Evidence points decidedly in that direction, but with some modifications. First, it is now clearly recognized that there are many causes or triggers for psychosis other than schizophrenia. Psychotic symptoms may appear as a result of, for example, advanced stages of HIV; amphetamine or cocaine overdose, which floods the brain with dopamine; severe depression, during which morbid hallucinations and delusions may appear; or extreme sensory deprivation, to name just a few. In other words, psychosis is a *syndrome*, a set of co-occurring features that appear in concert with one another but without a single, underlying cause. Certainly, schizophrenia is a disorder in which psychotic symptoms are salient, but bipolar disorder is similar in this regard, when the episodes become severe.

Note, in addition, that schizophrenia is not always characterized by clear psychosis. Rather, extreme lack of motivation and aversion to social contact, the so-called negative or deficit symptoms of schizophrenia, are likely to be prominent in between the periods of more florid psychosis. Overall, there is little evidence for Bleuler's perspective, which holds that psychosis inevitably signals schizophrenia.

Second, family history of mental disorder appears to validate the distinction. In general, schizophrenia and thought disorders cluster together in certain families, whereas unipolar depression and bipolar disorder characterize other "pedigrees." This distinction is not fail-safe, but it can be a helpful guide.

Third, the most compelling evidence for the distinction pertains to treatment response. Bipolar disorder is treatable with medications like lithium, and more recently carbamazepine and divalproex, agents that not only reduce manic symptoms but, more importantly, serve to prevent new manic and depressed episodes from occurring or from reaching their former levels of severity. Lithium is the best-documented of these medications with respect to a prophylactic or preventive effect regarding future episodes.[20] Schizophrenia, on the other hand, usually does not show response to lithium; rather, its symptoms are treated with a variety of antipsychotic medications. Most of the traditional antipsychotic medications reduce psychotic features regardless of the underlying diagnosis. That is, they can help with amphetamine overdoses, with psychotic symptoms accompanying depression and mania, as well as with schizophrenia per se. Indeed, antipsychotic medications can be a helpful treatment for certain persons with bipolar disorder, particularly during periods of florid psychosis. But these medications do not appear to serve any kind of preventive function with respect to the emergence of new mood episodes, and they work primarily on the psychotic features of mania or depression rather than on the mood-related symptoms.

Historic perspective may help to frame this discussion. For the first half of the last century, the field had no effective treatments for severe mental illness. Custodial care and sedation of one form or another – including barbaric interventions to keep patients chained or immobile – were the chief therapeutic alternatives. In the absence of efficacious intervention, there was no real impetus for diagnostic precision other than for reasons of recordkeeping or academic argument. Yet with the advent of more specific treatments, most notably, lithium as a preventive agent for manic-depression, accuracy in diagnosis became crucial.

Despite its discovery in the late 1940s in Australia as an antimanic agent, lithium was not utilized in the United States until the 1970s. Several reasons have been cited for its late acceptance. (1) Used indiscriminately, lithium can be highly toxic. Lithium chloride was promoted as a substitute for table salt in the late 1940s and early 1950s, but its use led to fatalities from lithium toxicity, stifling interest in this chemical just as its psychiatric properties were being discovered. It took years to overcome fears about using lithium, and its use in mood disorders still requires close monitoring.[21]

(2) Controlled trials of lithium's ability to treat and prevent bipolar cycles were difficult to implement, largely because of understandable ethical concern over the use of placebo-controlled studies for a disorder that can be lethal if left untreated. In Denmark, Dr. Mogens Schou courageously and creatively implemented experimental trials that were ethically defensible and scientifically sound; but it took until the late 1960s before such investigations were completed and

accepted.[22] Thus, over two decades transpired in the United States before lithium could be used for the treatment of manic-depressive illness.

(3) Given the Bleulerian model of major mental illness in this country, the prevalence of manic-depressive illness was believed to be quite low. Indeed, any manic or depressive episode that progressed to psychosis would inevitably receive a diagnosis of schizophrenia. Pharmaceutical firms were therefore reluctant to invest significant resources on a vanishingly rare condition that did not appear profitable. (So-called orphan drug laws have now been implemented, providing incentives for companies to manufacture and distribute medications for low-incidence conditions.) Relatedly, these companies were quite hesitant to promote a medication that could not be patented. Note that lithium is a natural element (number three on the periodic table), mined from the earth in salt form, rather than a manufactured compound.

Thus, the lack of diagnostic clarity in the field, along with safety and marketing concerns, served to delay the study and use of lithium. In turn, the slow adoption of lithium delayed important changes in the diagnostic system, as differential treatment response could not be recognized, perpetuating the belief that bipolar disorder was rare and diagnostically inconsequential.

This problem of misdiagnosis has had severe consequences. In the 1950s antipsychotic medications were discovered and rapidly marketed, witnessing a new era in the treatment of schizophrenia. Individuals like my father were treated with such medications, because no pharmacologic alternatives (other than pure sedation) existed and because the diagnosis of schizophrenia appeared to mandate their usage. These antipsychotic medications, the early generations of which were also termed neuroleptics or "major tranquilizers," control the symptoms of psychosis – agitation, thought disorder, hallucinations, delusions – regardless of the cause. They are a nonspecific, symptomatic intervention. Again, they still may be useful for the initial treatment of bipolar disorder. An individual presenting with psychotic-level mania may require antipsychotic treatment to decrease destructive, agitated behavior as well as hallucinations and delusions before more specific but slower-acting agents like lithium are introduced, at which time the antipsychotic medications can be tapered. In other words, lithium's actions are sufficiently slow that antipsychotics may be needed for initial control of the psychosis that typically accompanies stage 2 or 3 mania. Yet today, there would be few if any cases of bipolar disorder for which antipsychotic medications would be used exclusively and indefinitely, as they were for my father.

Crucially, most neuroleptics yield significant risk for tardive dyskinesia or other disfiguring movement disorders, conditions that may last for years or a even a lifetime. Tardive dyskinesia involves the onset, following a period of antipsychotic treatment (hence the name "tardive," signifying tardy or late onset), of uncomfortable and unsightly motor jerks and movements, often in the facial area. In a significant minority of cases, such movement disorders are a troubling accompaniment to treatment with these antipsychotic medications. The stigma of psychotic behavior is bad enough; the addition of distorted facial gestures or involuntary trunk movements compounds the individual's visible disturbance. Many thousands of individuals with severe mood disorders from the 1950s through the 1970s needlessly acquired such movement disorders as a function of misapplied antipsychotic medications. My father was fortunate to escape such a fate. Although the newer, "atypical" antipsychotic medications (e.g., clozapine, risperidone, olanzapine, quetiapine) yield a lower risk for such movement disorders, they have been available only relatively recently.

I must point out that reality does not always fall into neat divisions. Schizophrenia and mood disorders are not always clearly distinct at the level of symptoms, family histories (which may not fall out into separate pedigrees), or even long-term outcomes.[23] Indeed, directly counter to the claims of Kraepelin, it is now well known that substantial numbers of individuals with schizophrenia in fact show partial or even full recovery, directly countering the notion that schizophrenia is always associated with poor outcome.[24] The newest generation of atypical antipsychotic medications has also proven remarkably successful for a number of individuals with formerly chronic schizophrenia, belying the notion that afflicted persons are doomed to live the rest of their lives on back wards.

Likewise, mood disorders are not always purely episodic;[25] and in severe unipolar depression or bipolar disorder, functioning does not always revert to normal levels during the euthymic periods in between cycles. Particularly as the individual accrues a longer history of manic or depressed episodes over the years, there may be residual problems in memory and cognitive functioning that permeate the interepisode period.[26] Although it is difficult to tease apart my father's long history of episodes versus his regimen of inappropriate treatments with respect to understanding his gradual decline in mental functioning, his case appears to illustrate this phenomenon of gradual deterioration following a long history of mood cycles.

In sum, despite the arguments that I have raised regarding the distinction between schizophrenia and bipolar disorder, the lines are not clearly or cleanly drawn. Until more precise genetic markers are found and until more specific risk factors for each disorder are uncovered, there will not be the precise demarcation that would ensure complete diagnostic accuracy or specificity. Yet the disorders are typically distinguishable, if sound assessment and diagnostic procedures are followed.

Diagnostic Accuracy

To generate an accurate diagnosis of bipolar disorder, or any psychiatric or medical disorder, clinicians must go beyond the presenting symptoms and obtain a thorough history, appraise patterns of functioning over time, and consider such additional information as family history of functioning and illness. How is this done?

For one thing, accurate evaluation requires (as noted earlier) that the clinician obtain information from family members and other informants, as the patient's own disorganization and limited insight can severely limit the quality of his or her own report, particularly during active episodes. Family members can also provide information on psychiatric disturbance, hospitalizations, and treatment responses of biological relatives. Reliance on a single interview with the afflicted individual clearly will not suffice.

Also, structured interviews may be required. Unlike the traditional clinical interview, which may be quite open-ended as it follows the patient's lead, a structured interview contains highly organized lists of symptoms, about which the clinician asks in predetermined order and with standardized questioning. By this means, all of the relevant information about mood disorders, thought disorders, and many other symptom areas can be obtained with high consistency and with full coverage.

In addition, a full medical evaluation is often mandatory, in order to rule out the many types of physical conditions, medication side effects, and even infections of the brain that can yield mood- and thought-disordered symptoms. More specific laboratory markers – and, in the future, genetic markers[27] – play a role in diagnosis as well. Yet overall, there is no substitute for the thorough, careful gathering of information from validated interviews, checklists, and histories, from the patient and from informants who know the relevant history.

100

The key point is that because of the clearly lethal nature of untreated bipolar disorder, because of the hellish consequences that it yields for patients and family members, and because of the specific treatments that are available, precision in diagnosis is of paramount importance. Indeed, I often wonder how my father escaped suicidal behavior, given his long-standing misdiagnosis and the inadequate and inappropriate treatments he received as a result. Without university tenure, it is highly unlikely that he would have kept regular employment, given his erratic, irrational bursts of disorganized activity. Despite his gradual deterioration over the years related to his misdiagnosed and poorly treated episodes, he was in many respects fortunate that his outcome was not far worse: He survived, maintained a career and family, and avoided suicide and long-term side effects such as tardive dyskinesia.

Despite the field's vastly improved knowledge in recent years, the battle against impressionistic thinking and lack of attention to proper research must continue to be fought. Paul Meehl's classic 1973 article, "Why I Do Not Attend Case Conferences," portrays the flawed, nonskilled thinking that has for too long existed in the clinical enterprise.[28] For example, without comprehending the serious limitations that all humans (including clinicians) display with regard to interpersonal judgement and prediction, diagnosticians are prone to utilize initial impressions rather than precise formulas and to use outdated "rules" learned years ago rather than more up-to-date scientific information and valid assessment procedures. They may also fail to take into account accurate norms of behavioral and emotional functioning and to neglect asking about sensitive areas of inquiry like suicidal thoughts or plans, tendencies toward substance use and abuse, or extremely deviant behavior.

The issues I raise may appear be straightforward and obvious. After all, who would argue against care and precision

101

in diagnosis? Is there really opposition to this position? The answer, depressingly, is that that many critics show strong antipathy toward psychological and psychiatric evaluation and diagnosis. Indeed, classification in general is still the object of ridicule.[29] An "antipsychiatry" movement continues to exist, with some claiming that mental illness is simply a societal construct used to brand social deviance and others even contending that bipolar disorder is a misapplied medical label for what is essentially a lifestyle choice.[30] Even among more levelheaded clinicians and scientists, there may be a strong tendency to avoid diagnosing and therefore pathologizing disturbances in such basic human functions as emotions. After all, the symptoms of mania and depression clearly exist on a continuum with normal moods,[31] and resistance is often strong to label such emotional reactions and responses.

Yet, as revealed by rapidly accumulating genetic, psychobiological, and psychiatric evidence, as well as countless case histories, mood disorders are unquestionably real. Cavalier attitudes toward their evaluation and accurate diagnosis must be countered through enhanced professional education, through support of basic science and its linkages to the clinical enterprise, and through careful screening, training, and supervision of persons who pursue the mental health professions. A humanistic, holistic approach to patient care is fully compatible with more, rather than less, emphasis on diagnostic precision and rigor and on the use of assessment methods that can help to pinpoint differential diagnoses.

At the same time, the diagnostic categories currently in use are far from perfect. The scientific study of psychopathology has only recently emerged from infancy into an active childhood; maturity is still in the distant future. The diagnostic categories in the current guidebooks such as DSM are quite static, in that they condense the myriad symptoms, coping strategies, hope, fears, and struggles of the afflicted individual into a single diagnostic label. Lost in this perspective are the dynamic, ever-changing nature of the symptom picture, the intertwined nature of the person's symptoms and impairments with his or her core personality and strengths, and the inter-relationship between the individual's problematic functioning and his or her family, work, and community supports. In addition, diagnosis of a severe mental disorder typically fails to capture the unique features and even strengths that a given person brings to his or her problems and struggles. The act of classification may therefore mask the essential point that individuals with mental disorders comprise far more than their psychiatric diagnoses or labels. The more one interacts with those suffering from psychopathology, the more one learns from personal narratives, and the more one thinks deeply about one's own (or one's family's) deeply distressing experiences, the more difficult it is to stereotype persons afflicted with mental illness or to reduce them to simple diagnostic labels.

Still, accurate diagnosis is the cornerstone of initiating appropriate, empirically established treatments for individuals suffering from psychopathology. Although the affiliated mental health fields still have far to go in terms of establishing thorough and accurate evaluation practices that blend scientific rigor and concern for the individuality of each person being assessed, the struggle to do so is clearly worth the fight. Mental disorders are real, as I hope my father's history reveals, and ever-greater precision is a worthwhile goal.

As I resume the narrative, the decade of the 1970s is beginning. Change is in the air, in terms of both the classification of mental disorder in the United States and my father's stance of silence about his history.

8

Disclosure and New Diagnosis

It is December 1970. I have just turned eighteen and am back in Columbus for the Christmas holiday, on a two-week vacation from college. It feels strange to reexperience the house in which I grew up, as I reconsider my role within the family, thinking of how much I've changed in the past four months.

During the initial days of the holiday, I see friends from high school and spend some time studying, because my semester continues until the end of January. As Christmas day approaches, I want to give my Dad a gift that will be meaningful to him. I try to think of a book, instead of the standard present like a tie. I consider what I've read this fall and focus on a freshman seminar on "Social Deviance" that I've been taking. I suddenly think of a work by the British psychiatrist R. D. Laing, called The Divided Self.[1] *It is a work about the philosophical and existential dilemmas experienced by individuals undergoing the extreme psychoses of schizophrenia. I had been haunted by this work, which poignantly details the fragmentation of identity that is characteristic of this severe disorder, tying the struggles of afflicted individuals to core philosophical themes. I know of my father's having grappled with existential questions regarding life's meaning, and I know of his interest in the blend of psychology and philosophy.*

Disclosure and New Diagnosis

I sense that it is an important work, one that might challenge him.

On Christmas morning, as he unwraps the gift and looks at the title, his smile seems forced. Although he is cordial, and although there are more gifts to be opened, I sense that he is troubled. Consciously, at least, I am still in the dark about his history; yet I feel immediately that I've touched a nerve. I even overhear my mom and dad talking, in the next day or two, about why I'd given this book as a gift. Again, I sense that I'm too close to something important.

I am uneasy but I don't say anything. The holiday ends, and I return to Cambridge, Massachusetts, in early January, to prepare for the final exams and term papers that are coming up at the end of the month. I somehow can't approach my father to ask him about his unease over the gift.

The scene shifts to April 1971, a few months later. The spring semester has been a time of even more awakening for me than was the fall, and my head is full of ideas about literature, psychology, psychiatry, and the social sciences in general, as well as my own identity. What do I want to study? Pre-medicine or psychology? Would I ever be able to help people with psychological problems? How can I blend my interests in biology with those in the social sciences? Putting the questions aside for the time being, I fly home again for spring break.

A couple of days into my stay, my father asks me to his study, in this "new" house where we have lived since third grade, the year that he was absent. For this house, the study was designed at the outset, transcending the makeshift room in the basement of our old house, in which I had asked about the populations of Russia and China. It features built-in bookshelves across its length, stained a golden brown and lined with my father's extensive library. It is a room that is at once calming and stimulating, a soothing place to sit and read but also a setting that explodes with knowledge. I have always felt both thrilled and a bit overwhelmed entering that room, sensing that there is so much to learn from all those books that I find it hard to stop looking at all the titles and focus on just one.

My father sits at his large wooden desk near his manual type-writer, in this, his sanctuary. File folders full of course syllabi, notes on philosophical and scientific readings, and summaries of departmental meetings all crowd his desk. He is serious. I can tell that he wants to talk, not just about my year at college but about something more substantial. I feel nervous, both for myself and for him. What can he want to discuss?

He starts speaking softly and slowly. With a combination of seriousness and shyness, he begins awkwardly, with words to the effect that people sometimes have experiences in their lives that are hard for others to understand. The phrasing is in the third person, intellectualized and detached. But he then says, more clearly and personally, that he thinks that it might be time to let me know something of his life and his family's history. I hold my breath.

With rapt attention, I listen, still frightened but quite alert. He begins describing his nighttime journey in Pasadena, at age sixteen, framing it in terms of his fear of Nazi domination. He tells me that he was irrational, that he believed he must make a state-ment to stop Hitler. I am not used to this kind of disclosure from anyone in my family, particularly my father. I sense right away that very few people had ever heard him say such things. I know, before I can really understand why, that what he is telling me is central to his being, and to my own self as well.

Try as I might these years later, I can't recall the exact sequ-ence of this, our first talk. But in it he conveyed a sense of the Depression in Pasadena, of his brothers and early family life, again of his utter need to stop fascism, and of his hospitalization, hearing voices, sleeplessness, and fear. He said that he had experi-enced unusual thoughts at other points during his life, too. We didn't talk for too long, but he does say that he'd like to speak with me more, when there is time.

Disclosure and New Diagnosis

And so it began. Several times each year, at nearly every school break or holiday that I returned home, my father and I would find portions of one or two afternoons to return to the study, close the door, and resume our discussions. We would pick up on the last conversation and extend it to other themes. On other occasions, we would find a new direction. Or perhaps I would raise a question from the last talk. We spoke of his experiences in mental hospitals, his views on philosophy and psychology, his religious faith, his childhood, his college and graduate school years, his mother and his stepmother, and – frequently – the mysteries of our earth and of God. Several years later, as I learned more about bipolar disorder and began to sense that he had been misdiagnosed, our talks came to be more clinical in nature, focusing on his symptoms, his medications, his treatment planning. Other talks were freer flowing, dealing with historical themes, the essence of life, the nature of psychosis. The themes merged and remerged over the years.

When I think of the ebb and flow of our talks, I recall the liner notes from of an LP recording of one of Mahler's symphonies. I read these notes many years ago while listening to Mahler's music, during my early twenties, not long out of college. The text was beautifully written, stating that the movements of all of Mahler's symphonies were virtually interchangeable, that despite each symphony's independence and coherence, each movement was part of a lifelong musical vision.

So too with our talks: They now appear to me to be interchangeable, all part of a larger whole, which featured the many themes of my father's life and his vision of the world, all tied together despite the different strands of content.

Before each trip home, and during the initial hours and days of my return, I anticipated these talks with dread and fascination. I was afraid of what I might hear, and I felt nervous over the emotional intimacy of the contact. At the same time, I longed for the next talk. I was eager especially for the sense of learning about the realities of my family and my father that always took place. During and after each conversation, I had the sense of becoming much closer to my father as well as to a layer of reality that was deeper, more poignant, more attuned to the actual nature of the world than much of what I had learned from all of my other day-to-day conversations. I relished the stripping away of denial and confusion that our talks signified. The discussions were like windows on a world that I could scarcely imagine, linking me with my father's esoteric family out in California and with a set of experiences that I found simultaneously compelling, repulsive, and of the utmost significance.

On some trips, we would save our talk until it was time for my father to drive me to the airport to return to my new home. There, in the safety and privacy of the car and with the realization that we had at most a half an hour to speak, he began to open up even more.

I can sense now the anticipation when, in those moments preparing to talk, we would close the door of his study and resume our words. The trees through the windows might be barren in the winter, blossoming in the spring, or full during the summer, the books tender and red-hued in the dim light of the desk lamp, my mind filling with his words that described his most private experiences. These talks signaled my coming into adulthood and my awakening to the realities of my father, my family legacy, and my vision of who I was and who I might be in the world.

My parents and sister drove me from Ohio to New England in September of 1970, to start me off at Harvard. I was nervous about how the trip would go and whether it would be awkward saying goodbye to my family. But my anticipation of attending college back east outweighed such concerns. We headed through Pennsylvania, New York, and Connecticut, finally arriving in Massachusetts. Driving through the rainy streets of Boston and Cambridge, I realized that soon this new part of the world would be my home. The weather cleared; the early New England autumn was uplifting.

After a couple of days of exploring these new environs and getting unpacked in my dorm in Harvard Yard, we went out to dinner on my family's final night in town. Driving slowly back to Harvard Square, all of us knew that when I left the car, it would be into a new life. My father pulled the car up to the curb. I was anxious over the imminent goodbye but still eager to get started with this new experience of college, of independence.

The final words and hugs were tender, if a bit awkward. As I opened my door to depart, I noticed a pause up in the front seat. Looking hard, I noticed that my mother had suddenly and unexpectedly burst into tears. It was rare for her to display this kind of emotion. I was taken aback, not knowing what to do in order to console her, my heart nearly breaking. I realized only later that she couldn't really express the loss she felt and that I had been a real support to her throughout my childhood and adolescence, largely through my "holding it together," succeeding academically, and keeping stable. Even now, the memory of her tears is as vivid as though it happened within the past few weeks. I can hear her nearly inaudible sobs, see her shoulders shaking, and feel the alarm in my body and the lump in my throat. Although I sometimes wonder what I might have done to ease the pain, there was really nothing to do other than to proceed to the dorm and begin my new life. I couldn't repair my father's history, about which I knew so little, or fill in the holes in my mother's years of coping, or stay frozen in time back in high school.

I quickly became immersed in life at Harvard. Although I was a Midwesterner amidst a deluge of New England prep school graduates, I learned that I could hold my own in classes. I even played football for the freshman team, though it wasn't nearly as exciting as our high school state championship days.

The campus, as well as Boston and Cambridge in general, opened up new worlds for me. I was stimulated and intellectually excited. I realized, quickly, how paltry my knowledge was of the fields in which I was interested. I hungrily explored various aspects of psychology, as well as literature and social theory, fueled by the talks I would have with my father during my periodic visits home.

I had a vague sense of wanting to go to medical school and pursue psychiatry. But by my sophomore year, I had become engaged in several volunteer experiences: working as a Big Brother, teaching in a Massachusetts prison, serving as a home-based therapist for a young adolescent as part of a community mental health center treatment team. Through such volunteer experiences, I consolidated my desire to continue in the field of psychology, realizing that I was getting more out of this kind of work than by slogging through pre-medical courses.

During the summers, I stayed in New England, first to work as a tutor at a residential school for children with learning disabilities and then to serve as a counselor at a camp for developmentally disabled children. These experiences prepared me clinically to work with children and families and to interact with large staffs of volunteers, professionals, and researchers. They also left me stimulated intellectually, with a press to understand far more about causes and treatments of various mental and developmental disorders.

My father began a regular habit of mailing me reprints of articles in psychology, philosophy, medicine, and related fields, in order to keep me current, to share what he thought was interesting from what he was reading. These letters and mailings during the academic year – a key chapter here, an article from *Science* that he had found particularly interesting there – came to supplement our talks in Columbus during my vacations as a way of connecting both intellectually and emotionally.

I soon stopped trying out for varsity sports teams and concentrated on my academic courses as well as my volunteer work in the field of psychology. I was performing at a high level in my courses, but I still felt that I was missing the kind of incandescence and philosophical spark that my father had kindled in himself and experienced in college and graduate school.

In my senior year, my father became acutely symptomatic during the fall semester, requiring hospitalization. I picked up a few details from my mother, during calls home. On a night that I had been to the library studying, he had tried calling me from the psychiatric hospital where he was staying, but was only able to leave a message with a roommate, without a telephone number attached. To this day I regret not having been able to speak with him during that time. I wonder how he would have talked about himself and how he would have sounded. He did not stay long, however, as his episode peaked just beyond hypomania and was short-lived, without the destructive psychosis of past episodes.

Although my academic work at college was quite good, although my mind was filling with exciting ideas, and although I was gaining valuable experience in my volunteer work and summer jobs, I was far from being at peace during this time. Most tellingly, I began to have trouble sleeping on a number of nights, both from academic pressures and from vaguer worries about what my father's disclosures really meant. What was my risk for psychosis or schizophrenia? I wondered to myself. How controlled did I need to be in my life? What if I can't fall asleep – what then? Might I somehow lose control and become symptomatic?

I also began to read more, starting to question whether my father's history of episodes really fit the criteria for schizophrenia. This was the early 1970s, when the disregard for diagnostic precision in American psychiatry and clinical psychology was just beginning to turn the corner toward neo-Kraepelinian views. At Harvard, however, this movement was still years away. My questions to professors about the differential diagnosis between schizophrenia and manic-depressive illness were met with blank expressions. In addition, when I went to Health Services about my occasional, but severe, migraine headaches, which would lead to terrible pain and uncontrolled nausea, I was given outmoded psychodynamic formulations. For example, I told one physician that glare from sunlight appeared to me to be a strong trigger for these types of headaches. Deriding my inaccuracy, he told me scornfully that a person may believe, upon (for example) departing a movie theater, that the glare outside may have triggered a migraine headache; but the emotional content of the film itself was, of course, the real cause.

On more and more nights, now several times a month, my insomnia began to trigger a kind of panic: What if I couldn't sleep at all? Would I stay up all night and not be able to function the next day? Might I then begin to develop symptoms such as those my father had begun to discuss with me during vacations? As I lay awake, I would also sense that I couldn't clear my throat or stomach of mucus that was accumulating. Part of this sensation had begun to arise in the past few years, following a football injury in ninth grade when someone I was trying to tackle had accidentally stepped on my nose underneath the face guard of my helmet. The resultant deviated septum made breathing difficult. Now in college, and unable to sleep, I would begin to feel nauseous from the congestion, and, with increasing desperation, I would recall the events that would transpire when a migraine headache got to its worst phases.

Disclosure and New Diagnosis

Nearly all of the men in my father's family – my grandfather, my father, and all of his full brothers – as well as my maternal grandmother and my sister had experienced "classic" migraines such as mine, in which an aura of flashing lights and loss of vision in one visual field would be followed by piercing pain on the other side of my head, with the pain lasting for many hours. Mine began when I was eleven, when I lost vision during a hot, glare-filled spring afternoon and had to go home to recover. Each time, intense nausea would accompany the headache, leading to severe, uncontrollable vomiting, sometimes for hours. During some of the migraines, I would become confused and even aphasic, temporarily losing speech. On several occasions I needed to go to the emergency room. Mercifully, such migraines never occurred more than a few times a year, but they left a lasting impact on me and my sense of vulnerability.

At college, on the nights that my sleeplessness, nausea, and fear were most intense, I would despair of ever falling asleep. One night I resorted to a strategy that had, of necessity, worked when a migraine headache got into its worst phases. At those times, as I would vomit uncontrollably, relief would finally come when all of the contents of my stomach (even bile and blood) would be released. Sometimes, however, I was so exhausted from throwing up that I would need to induce the remaining acts of vomiting by gagging myself. Once I had finished, the feeling of relief was, despite my exhaustion, palpable, because then I could lie in bed and finally fall asleep, to awaken hours later with the headache gone.

Recalling those moments at the end of a migraine, I embarked upon a strategy: I would lift myself from my sleepless bed, go into the bathroom, and try to induce vomiting, not of any food (which long since had been digested) but of accumulated mucus and bile. I was searching for a parallel to that blessed moment near the end of a migraine when I had

113

finally purged my stomach of all contents and could relax, knowing that the nausea would abate and sleep would finally come.

In this way, I gradually became convinced that the only way to clear the congestion and ease the discomfort during those restless nights was to make myself vomit. It wasn't a pattern of bulimia, in that no food would be lost, only dry heaves or some mucus or bile. Sometimes I would drink water before I began the process in order to have something in my stomach to regurgitate. I would be tired, but relieved, the next morning, and the pattern would abate for a couple of weeks. But the problem grew in frequency as well as intensity. By the end of my college years, it had become an issue several nights each month.

I began to alter my life to accommodate this ritual. The mornings following these bouts, I would look drawn from the exhaustion of the vomiting and the lack of sleep. It became difficult to think of how I could get to the bathroom at night, alone and away from others, if I took a trip or stayed over at someone's house. I didn't tell anyone about this problem, for fear of embarrassment. I noted to my parents and some friends that I had a problem related to congestion and that sometimes I would vomit, but I didn't go into the real nature of the issue.

Despite these growing nighttime problems, I continued to do well in my courses and remained appreciative of my expanding physical and social world in Boston and Cambridge, my growing intellectual world in psychology, and my increasing concerns with social issues related to prison reform and mental health. But I felt as though I led a split life: in good energy throughout much of every day, but increasingly worried about loss of control at night.

I graduated with highest honors in 1974. I was elected to Phi Beta Kappa, and I received the singular honor of receiving the Ames Award, which was awarded to the senior who best blended academic success with social action. From my summertime jobs working at therapeutic summer camps, I had gained sufficient experience that I was able to obtain a paid job in the fall, serving as coordinator of a small day school program for developmentally disabled children and adolescents in Boston. I oversaw the classrooms, conducted parent management courses, supervised the teachers, hired and trained volunteers, and consulted with the psychologists and psychiatrists back at Massachusetts Mental Health Center who had obtained the funding and space for the school. In addition, the following year I was asked to direct the residential camp in New Hampshire for children with severe emotional and developmental disabilities where I had served as counselor for two summers and then as program director for a third. Here, I took on roles similar to those at the school program, but with a much larger staff and with the responsibility of round-the-clock care of severely impaired children at a rural summer camp location. At both programs, I learned to fundraise and to coordinate research activities. I knew that I would eventually attend graduate school, but I was eager to do real work in the field, and these were tremendous opportunities.

The summer camp directorship also afforded me the opportunity to explore the lakes and mountains of New Hampshire through canoeing and hiking. I was in my element. Yet I was in my own "bipolar" world: taking on increasing responsibility for the lives of children in two different programs, each intensive and loaded with responsibility, while at the same time grappling at night with an increasing sense of being out of control, at the mercy of my sleeplessness, fears, and forced vomiting in order to obtain any relief. Things came to a head during my second year out of college, when the nighttime rituals became increasingly frequent. Several times per week, I couldn't relax and, fueled by the belief that the only way to

115

get any sleep was to clear my system, began the procedure of forced vomiting. The strain, physical exhaustion, and mental anguish were rapidly accumulating.

Around this time, however, I began a new relationship, and I told my partner of my worries and rituals. Having them be less of a secret was a big step. During the middle of the fall, I had a quiet realization one night that perhaps I could just relax and wait out the feeling of nausea. I quietly reasoned to myself that I might be able to transcend the discomfort and eventually fall asleep, without any need to purge. There was no magical insight, just a kind of hunch, a letting go of the desperate need for control that had been building. Somehow, my intuition paid off: I waited out the feeling of congestion and nausea and eventually did fall asleep. Fueled by this success, within a week or two the problem had abated. I then sought out behavior therapy, which, through relaxation and imagery, helped me to maintain this realization and fight the feelings of unease and vague nausea that sometimes returned.

How could this self-destructive pattern of behavior have become so severe? The "behaviorist" side of me believes that these episodes were the result of a kind of superstitious conditioning, in which I came to associate the real relief brought on by involuntary vomiting during a migraine with the need to perform the same act in another stressful circumstance, that of failing to fall asleep. I came to rely on a conditioned strategy that wasn't needed, but I had become too locked in to give it up, even after it had begun to take on an increasingly destructive role.

From another vantage point, more "dynamic" in nature, I see the issues as deeper, perhaps reflecting a form of separation anxiety (being away from my family of origin) and also recapitulating the sleeplessness and need for control during third grade when my father was gone for the year. There was also, of course, a strongly self-punitive aspect to my rituals. Perhaps at some level I was trying to purge myself of what I was learning about my family legacy. And the harshness of my method of inducing relaxation was a signal of the depth of the struggle inside. It is hard for me to imagine, with hindsight, that I allowed myself to get so locked in to this destructive pattern. Luckily, I rather suddenly developed the faith that I simply didn't need to continue the purging, and the pattern halted abruptly in the wake of that faith.

Overall, there are undoubtedly both conditioned and deeper emotional aspects to my development of this pattern of behavior. Similarly, there are both behavioral and more dynamic aspects to my letting go of it, reflected in both the simple act of stopping the behavior plus the more ineffable attaining of the inner strength and faith to realize that I could do so.

The following winter, feeling really healthy for the first time in a number of years, I resigned as coordinator of the school program to devote more attention to directing the summer residential camp. With free time in the early spring, I drove cross-country to California, partly related to work and partly for the adventure of the trip. While at the University of California, Los Angeles (UCLA), where I had academic contacts, I made sure to visit my father's brothers in the area.

I was especially eager to see my Uncle Bob, the psychiatrist, to discuss my father. Despite Bob's need for home dialysis related to kidney failure, secondary to his substance abuse from years earlier, he was glad to see me. I recall his serious but pleased tone as he asked me whether I had done as well at Harvard as my father had recounted to him over the telephone.

I immediately trusted him and told him of my increasing conviction that Dad had manic-depressive illness, not schizophrenia, and that he needed lithium, rather than Mellaril. I had been drawing these conclusions based on my reading, and I took the risk of confronting my uncle directly about these issues. He immediately voiced shock that my father had not already been receiving lithium. He had reached the same conclusions as I, but he had not communicated them to my father. I surmised that the two brothers were not as close as they had been years before and suspected that my father, perhaps out of shame that his brother had needed to rescue him several times, hadn't been keeping up much contact. Perhaps Bob's increasing health problems had prevented him from reaching out to my father as well.

Regardless, I was relieved that his clinical judgment matched mine. Shortly after my visit, Bob contacted my father's psychiatrist, who had coincidentally just received continuing medical education about bipolar disorder and lithium treatment. The psychiatrist immediately discontinued the Mellaril and began to prescribe lithium. My father obtained regular blood checks for this new treatment, which are mandatory for a person beginning this regimen. Also, partly at my urging, he began to read considerably about bipolar disorder and its treatments. After nearly forty years, he had a new diagnosis and a treatment that was tailored specifically to it.

The medication helped: No episodes ensued for a number of years. Indeed, my father was quite thankful for a degree of assurance that he would not suddenly begin to experience psychosis. He read eagerly about his new diagnosis, which became the subject of many of our continuing conversations when I would return home.

Yet he was also quite prone to certain side effects from the lithium. He voiced considerable concern over the fine-motor tremor that impaired his elegant handwriting, and he seemed to have inordinate trouble with frequent nightly urination. His blood levels stayed in the low ends of the therapeutic range, as he stabilized on dosage levels that were smaller than the norm.

Just before this time, in 1975, my mother began to develop severe pain in her joints, initially diagnosed as bursitis but quickly recognized by specialists as rheumatoid arthritis. Thus, just as she turned fifty, she began to suffer from this progressive, painful affliction, which precipitated multiple regimens of medications as well as several surgeries for her hands and feet over the past quarter-century. She has borne this affliction with tremendous courage. I can only speculate how much the origins of this disease were related to her years of silent coping with my father's episodes and unpredictability. I do know that physicians have suggested this same opinion to her.

Visits to the family home, which I continued to make several times per year, were complex. I continued to get along well with my father, mother, and sister, and I relished the talks my father and I would have. Yet I despaired over my father's occasional depressions (despite the overall success of the lithium treatment, the medication did not prevent the flat, empty moodstates that still emerged periodically), his slow but now perceptible decline in cognitive functioning, and my mother's rapidly developing arthritis. I tried to caretake each of them, but my efforts always fell short. When I would leave to return to New England, or subsequently to California for graduate school, I felt guilty for not having accomplished more, asking myself how I was able to get away from this tangled web of problems and whether it was really fair that I did not stay longer and help out more. I was experiencing a kind of survivor guilt, a sense of unease at my escape from this set of difficulties.

With increasing conviction, I was deciding that my future career should be in clinical psychology, a profession that would allow me to blend basic research on causes of mental disorders with applied research on treatment-related efforts. During my third year after college, I applied to and was accepted at several doctoral programs and decided on UCLA, because of its excellent reputation. In the fall of 1977 I flew cross-country to begin my new life as a graduate student. An added benefit was that I would now be closer to my father's brothers.

Although graduate school can certainly be a stressful experience, I recall thinking what a luxury and a joy it was to start my graduate studies. I remember my first weeks in Los Angeles, a bit disoriented by the daily sunshine, warm weather, and smog, but amazed that I had a fellowship that allowed me to take courses in assessment, psychopathology, psychopharmacology, research design, and clinical theories without the strain of conducting a summer camp or coordinating a school program. What a gift, I thought, to be able to read and study and to receive clinical supervision. I took as many courses as I could.

During my first year, my Uncle Bob's health was continuing to fail. That winter, he was recommended for a kidney transplant. He lived not far from the UCLA campus, and I was quite concerned for his well-being. I immediately sought consultation regarding the advisability of my father's serving as a kidney donor.

I had heard that a young, brilliant expert on bipolar disorder named Kay Jamison worked at the UCLA medical center, and I subsequently heard her deliver an inservice talk at our Psychology Clinic. I called her up and set up a meeting. Without any formal introduction to me at all, she listened to the situation over the phone and quickly agreed to meet. In her office, located somewhere in the maze of the vast UCLA medical complex, she listened attentively and provided up-to-date information on the kidney-related side effects of lithium and on bipolar disorder in general. I was as impressed with her generous giving of time as with her authoritative knowledge. I was hopeful that I could help my uncle, while ensuring that my father could safely serve as a donor.

Disclosure and New Diagnosis

Although I was hoping that my father would decide to donate, he ultimately decided against doing so, on the basis of medical advice he had received that it might be too risky to have a single kidney while continuing to receive lithium treatment. It was not until the next fall that my uncle received a cadaver kidney that was a suitable match. The operation was scheduled, and for several weeks afterward the new kidney functioned well. I visited Bob in the hospital and saw the animated, jovial man that I had remembered from my childhood visits to California. He was aided by the high dosages of steroids prescribed to fight tissue rejection. In fact, he became nearly hypomanic from the steroid regimen, a reaction that is not atypical with high dosage levels.

Several days later, however, he quickly declined and died from complications related to the rejection process. I was stunned. A number of questions circulated in my mind: Why had my uncle, so promising a psychologist and psychiatrist, succumbed to self-injected analgesic medications, initially triggered by the attempt to control severe migraine-related pain? Was this ultimately fatal substance abuse somehow related to my father's bipolar disorder? How had he and my father become so disconnected over the years? What did my father owe to this brother, who had consoled him as a child after severe punishments from their stepmother and who had, decades later, flown out to admit him to mental hospitals and then ensured his treatment with lithium following my own outreach? How I wish that Bob had lived longer, so that I could have asked him more about my father's initial episodes, about his own developing interest in mental health, and his road through life.

My father immediately flew to Los Angeles for the funeral, as he had done three years earlier for the funeral of his oldest brother. He stayed with me in my apartment near Venice Beach, reminiscing about his Pasadena childhood and his

121

escapades with his brother, half a century before. We drove around Los Angeles and Malibu, witnessing the aftermath of the seasonal fires that had scorched the dried trees during the hot autumn winds. My father was sad, incredulous that his beloved but distanced brother was really gone, but he appeared to be managing his emotions philosophically. He reiterated to me that taking lithium made him feel safe in ways that he had never experienced before.

A year and a half later, during a visit to California by my parents, I noticed a subtle but detectable "breakthrough" hypomania in my father. This term refers to an episode that occurs (or "breaks through") despite one's taking lithium or other prophylactic medication. His treating physician back in the Midwest had been cavalier regarding the monitoring of my father's lithium levels, which had slipped below the therapeutic range. My father's mood continued to surge throughout the fall, but he remained at stage 1 of mania and did not require hospitalization. Whether this episode was "capped" by the low levels of lithium in my father's bloodstream or would have peaked at hypomanic levels on their own, I cannot say.

I was thriving in graduate school, becoming increasingly interested in child clinical psychology and developmental psychopathology, the study of the relationship between normal and atypical development. But graduate school days in California also afforded another kind of learning, as evidenced by a chance discussion I had, during my second year, when I went to a travel agency to purchase airline tickets for a trip to San Francisco. Standing at the counter, I gave my name to confirm the reservation. The agent stared at me and said: " . . . Hinshaw, Hinshaw . . . Hey, I know that name. Are you related to _____? [He stated a first name that I didn't recognize.] You related to this guy? He lives out east of L.A. He's the one who hears voices that aren't there! Wacked out guy – way out there!"

Disclosure and New Diagnosis

There aren't too many Hinshaws around, and the young man to whom he was referring must undoubtedly be a distant relative. Learning in this offhand way about a relative reinforced my vulnerability. It also fueled my sense of being an unwitting survivor, through fate or fortune, of the family legacy of mental disorder. Again, I asked myself how I had escaped – or indeed whether I *had* fully escaped, at this point in my life.

During my graduate school years, I also reencountered the two first cousins (the sons of my father's half-brothers) whom I described in Chapter 1. I could hardly believe the devastating destructiveness of their respective conditions. I learned that one cousin, who had attended Berkeley but never returned after his schizophrenia became severe, had subsequently spent much time in the L.A. beach community of Venice, where I now lived. He was known, in the mid-1970s, for his flowing beard and his delusion that he was Jesus. He now lived in a board-and-care home south of Los Angeles, which was, in reality, a converted, ugly, motel-like structure in a tough neighborhood. He inconsistently took the antipsychotic medications that the consulting psychiatrist would prescribe on sporadic visits to the facility. Through contact with his father, my uncle Paul, I took him out driving a couple of times, but it was clear that he was still delusional, and a deep connection was difficult to make.

During one family reunion at Uncle Paul's home, my parents were in California visiting me. I saw my father in an intense conversation out in the yard with my cousin, who delusionally insisted that he was the Messiah. My father, however, didn't back down, using his religious training and his status as a former mental patient to try and talk more sense into him.

The other cousin had been living most of his life back in Nebraska, where he had been raised. He had clearly experienced both manic highs and depressive lows; but in between these episodes, he remained thought-disordered and delusional. He thus suffered from what is called schizoaffective disorder, a severe, puzzling condition that blends many of the worst aspects of bipolar disorder and schizophrenia. He had a sweet, innocent quality. Yet several years after I last saw him on a visit he had made to California with his parents, he committed suicide.

Seeing my cousins, trying to relate to them, and contemplating their fates raised a number of questions. What would life be like to be delusional most of the time? Why were they afflicted, and not I? How had I escaped such a plight? And how could I reconcile the talents, skills, and relative stability I seemed to possess with their life courses? I still wonder at the luck of the genetic draw with which people are born.

I also note in passing that, because these cousins of mine are sons of my father's half-brothers, it may be the case that their propensity for schizophrenia-spectrum disorders emanated from my step-grandmother's side of the family, whereas risk for mood disorder was transmitted through my grandfather's side. This possible situation, that the risks for schizophrenia versus mood disorder were being transmitted independently in my family tree, is consistent with genetic theories that view these conditions as at least partially separable.

At this point in my life, in my mid- to late twenties, I didn't have much of a desire to have children. Although I had never had any semblance of mania or psychosis, I still worried what I might be transmitting to a child. Only with the passage of time and the cultivation of a long-term relationship, in the next few years, did such worries about parenthood diminish.

Throughout this period, I was glad that I could continue to communicate with and help my father. My increasing knowledge about psychopathology from graduate courses allowed me to be more informative to him. My parents had begun to come to Palm Springs each winter, eventually purchasing a townhouse, which afforded me greater opportunity to continue my talks with my father. Whenever he would come to California or whenever I would return to Ohio, our talks would resume, as before, and they increasingly included new information that he or I had obtained about mental disorder, lithium, and other treatments. The talks continued to nurture us both, as the content developed and evolved in tandem with my father's new diagnosis and treatment regimen and with my expanded knowledge of both the field and myself. After more than a decade, the talks had become a fixture of our relationship.

9
Waning Powers

It is February, 1982, in Los Angeles. Usually, winter in Southern California means occasional rainstorms that quickly clear the air, with a return to the predominant sunshine. But this winter has been particularly wet: an El Niño winter, before the term became popular. My father's visit has yielded more clouds and rain than sun.

I have finished four years of graduate school and am now a clinical psychology intern at the Neuropsychiatric Institute of UCLA, one of the premier psychiatry departments in the country. The training opportunities are so plentiful that it's hard to choose which rotations to take. The learning is nonstop. The fellow interns are stimulating, and several of us have become close friends. Perhaps my finest learning experience is taking place at the Affective Disorders Clinic, a specialty clinic for the assessment and treatment of patients with severe unipolar depression and bipolar disorder. The clinic is directed by Kay Jamison, with whom I had consulted several years before, as a first-year graduate student, about my uncle and my father.

Midway through the academic year, the clinic is sponsoring an erudite symposium on advances in the treatment of bipolar disorder. Featured speakers are Frederick Goodwin, soon to be director of the National Institute of Mental Health, and Mogens

Waning Powers

Schou, the Danish psychiatrist who did the essential clinical trials on lithium during the 1950s and 1960s, convincing the world that it was a viable prophylactic treatment for bipolar disorder. In anticipation of the event, I call my father, who, now in partial retirement, has the time to come to California and attend. He flies out, both to continue his own learning about his condition and to spend some time with me. He will spend a week with me at my apartment before my mother makes the journey and they both head on to Palm Springs.

The symposium is, in fact, most impressive, with presentations on genetics, biological underpinnings of bipolar disorder, and the role of lithium as well as support group therapy in preventing episodes. It is clear that the symposium and the sponsoring Affective Disorders Clinic are at the vanguard of knowledge in the field. Although not always alert for the entire session, given his tendency to drift off during long talks, my father enjoys the meeting and appears to gain knowledge from the interchange of ideas.

A couple of days later, I am busy one day at the internship, while my father explores Venice, the beach community in Los Angeles where I live, known for attracting artistic and noncon-ventional types. He spends much of the day walking on the beaches and going to cafes. The winter sky is alternately cloudy and sunny, the sparkling blue of the Pacific alternating with gray, heavy waves.

When I return to my apartment that evening, I ask him about his day. He describes his enjoyment of Southern California, where he grew up, and the colorful scene at Venice Beach. At one cafe, where he had eaten some lunch, he describes sitting near several "interesting characters" and tells me that he could immediately tell that some of them had been hospitalized in facilities for mental patients. "When you've been in mental hospitals as much as I have," he explains, "you can spot the psychotics like yourself right away."

I am stunned, not knowing how to respond. Have I heard him correctly? Has he not just attended the elite symposium at UCLA and learned that bipolar disorder is a highly heritable, biologically based condition? Hasn't he "owned" his rediagnosis as a person who was afflicted with this disorder? Apparently, his largely successful treatment with lithium and his book knowledge of manic-depressive illness have failed to put a dent in his underlying self-image: that of "a psychotic," an inmate of hospitals.

A few days later, my mother arrives in California. Each day, however, Dad has seemed increasingly distant and "out of it," more tired and confused and with a tremor in his hand that is worse than usual. I secretly wish to myself that he weren't so compliant with his lithium, as it's seeming to dull him out. Within two days, his condition worsens precipitously – he can barely use his keys to open doors because of his confusional state. The next evening, at my parents' hotel room, he becomes sick to his stomach and vomits. I arrange, hurriedly, for him to be seen at the Affective Disorders Clinic the next morning, where his lithium serum level is found to be at the highest end of the normal range, in stark contrast to his usual low to normal readings. This reading would probably have been even higher had he not vomited some of his evening's dosage the previous night.

In short, he is experiencing lithium toxicity. With consultation from the highly skilled Affective Disorders Clinic staff, he discontinues the medication and quickly "clears." I realize, however, that his doctor back in Columbus hasn't been monitoring him carefully, and that treatment with lithium, especially for older individuals, is not a casual affair.

Will it ever get easier?

My father was vice-chair of the Ohio State Philosophy Department for a number of years, in the 1960s and 1970s. Much of his work was therefore administrative, supplementing his teaching load. Original, scholarly publications were by that time few and far between. His occasional talk of organizing his papers and ideas into one or more books – talk that would increase when symptoms of hypomania became apparent – was clearly not going to happen.

Often he would seem tired, too tired, after a day's work; colleagues reported that he would regularly close his eyes and drift into a nap during afternoon faculty meetings. Each night he would, per prescription, take a portion of a sleeping pill; late each afternoon he would try to take a real nap, once he returned home. The years of out-of-control cycles, of various medications, and now even the lithium, were all taking a toll on his mental alertness.

In 1981, as I was finishing my fourth year of graduate school, he opted for an early retirement package from the university, which allowed him to stay on with a reduced teaching load at age sixty-two (with thirty-five years of continuous service under his belt) while vacating his tenured slot. In the letter he wrote to the dean requesting this status, he was extremely gracious, stating his concern with university funding difficulties, which threatened the stability of assistant professors in the department. He thus wished to retire in order to assure their positions. I am sure, however, that he was aware of his waning academic productivity and that he was sensitive to the hints from colleagues that this might be an optimal move. He was too proud to speak of the underlying reasons openly.

The department scheduled a retirement symposium and dinner at Ohio State for the spring, and I made plans with my mother and sister to return home from California without telling him, in order to be a surprise attendee at the dinner celebration. I made the flight to Columbus from Los Angeles on a sultry spring evening, arriving with my sister via my grandmother's house, in order to preserve the surprise. I recall his shock and delight upon seeing me on the steps of the faculty club, facing the huge, grassy oval in the center of the campus, in the long twilight of the Midwest May evening. His

129

face showed incredulity that I had actually made the special trip.

The dinner was well attended and cordial, although I had the distinct sense that the honors were for someone who had peaked in his career many years before. Indeed, the department chair, a longtime friend and colleague of my father's, made a point of telling me privately that it had been increasingly difficult to support my father's staying on in a regular faculty slot during recent years, given his behavioral and emotional history and his lagging academic productivity.

I stayed in Columbus for the rest of the week. Within a day or so, I became aware that my father was in a depressed state. In fact, he seemed blank and unresponsive in the aftermath of the retirement dinner. I tried talking with him about my perceptions, but he dismissed my concerns, seemingly oblivious to the extent of his distance from the world. After driving him to his office one afternoon later in the week, I was in tears while returning to the family home, despairing that he was not really hearing me in my attempts to reach out to him and convey my concern over his depression. He just didn't seem to want to know. His level of insight was quite poor, thwarting my efforts to do something to help.

Once I returned to California, I wondered out loud during a phone conversation with him about his potentially receiving an antidepressant to supplement his lithium, which was now prescribed at extremely low dosages (one 300 mg pill per day) because of concerns over the side effects of tremor, increased urination, and lethargy. He raised the issue with his psychiatrist, who immediately started him on a then-new tetracyclic antidepressant medication, Ludiomil (mapratilone). I was surprised, upon hearing of this turn of events, that the physician prescribed a new and relatively untested agent so quickly.

From accounts of both of my parents, my father began almost immediately to experience an adverse set of reactions, including disorientation and a sudden deterioration of his eyesight, related to macular degeneration. Indeed, mapratilone is now seldom used, not only because of the advent of the selective serotonin reuptake inhibitors (SSRIs) such as Prozac, which became widely adopted several years later, but also because of its risks for precipitating macular degeneration. My attempt at involvement had clearly backfired. My father's psychiatrist discontinued the medication within a couple of weeks, and I was extremely reluctant to suggest medication changes again. Over the next months, his depressed state gradually lifted by itself.

Should I have been in the dual role of family member and advocate? Sometimes this sharing of responsibilities is inevitable, but problems can clearly emerge. I was frustrated with the continued passivity of both my father and his doctor, and I wanted to make something happen. With hindsight, I realize that I should have received more consultation before speaking out. Even today, blending antidepressant medication with lithium or other mood stabilizers for treatment-resistant bipolar depressions is a treatment option that does not automatically guarantee success.

I spent the following academic year in my internship at UCLA's Neuropsychiatric Institute, during which my father attended the symposium on bipolar disorder. My research back in the Psychology Department was focusing increasingly on children, but I was eager to participate in a well-balanced set of internship training experiences and therefore selected work in the specialties of schizophrenia aftercare, affective disorders, neuropsychology, family therapy, and other rotations. It was the most intellectually stimulating year of my life.

The rotation through the Affective Disorders Clinic was the highlight of the year. My knowledge of mood disorders increased dramatically. Among many revelations, one experience stands out. Jamison conducted a weekly seminar meeting of the clinic, with nearly twenty interns, residents, and staff members participating. These were lively sessions. At one meeting in the late fall, during a discussion of the genetics of mood disorders, Jamison asked the group to imagine a time in the future when a gene for bipolar disorder, or at least a gene that carried strong risk for bipolar disorder, might be detectable in the amniotic fluid. She asked the group: How many of you would elect to abort if it were your child with a positive detection?

To my disbelief, although my hand stayed glued to the table, nearly every other hand in the room shot up. How could this be the case, I thought to myself. Is this really the opinion of the staff and trainees of such a select, academic clinic? Is bipolar disorder this toxic, this noxious, or this devastating? Perhaps, I later reasoned, the vote might be explainable by the clinic's status as a tertiary-care, specialty setting, with much of its caseload composed of difficult-to-treat patients who had not responded to standard treatments in the community. In other words, perhaps the trainees and staff had seen only the most lithium-resistant, difficult, and intransigent cases, distorting their perceptions of the typical nature of bipolar disorder.

Even so, the vote still suggested a strong fear of mental illness, a strong sense of "us" versus "them," and a clear lack of belief in the effectiveness (or potential effectiveness) of preventive treatment strategies, all coming from educated trainees and professionals in training at a leading academic center. Did the staff not know of people like my father, I wondered, who have made it through life despite manic-depressive illness? Would my father have even been born had his parents, years before, been able to detect a genetic risk for his later episodes? Or what about me, with whatever genetic risk or loading I may have been found to "carry" while still in utero? What decision might my parents have been encouraged to make?

Given the rapid pace of genetic and genomic advances, such questions are increasingly salient today. What would be the ramifications for families, for society, and indeed for all of humankind if we choose to eliminate the genes underlying bipolar disorder? What about the creativity and achievement, in addition to the disorganization and despair, that often go together with the disorder? Unafflicted relatives of individuals with bipolar disorder tend to show considerable success in many areas of human endeavor, such as scientific accomplishment and artistic achievement.[1] Would overzealous elimination of genetic risk remove such propensities from the gene pool as well? A cascade of unintended effects might emanate from this new form of eugenics. Because the genetic risk for mood disorders is not simple or unitary in nature, we ought to be extremely cautious about premature attempts at its elimination; the ethics of psychiatric genetics is a topic that must continue to receive attention from the best minds in the field.

During the time of the symposium that my father attended, Mogens Schou, the Danish psychiatrist who performed the pathbreaking clinical trials that demonstrated the efficacy of lithium in combating bipolar disorder, spent two weeks at UCLA as a guest of the clinic. One afternoon, he gave a colloquium to the staff. From the many key points he made, I recall two clearly. First, he told of his insistence, years earlier, that his laboratory group (and he himself) take lithium for several months as they initiated their landmark investigations of its effects. With extreme gravity, he queried our psychiatric residents and fellows: "Would you actually prescribe a psychotropic medication that you had not yourself taken?" Indeed, he showed us the permanent, disfiguring psoriasis on his arm that resulted from his own trial of lithium self-medication, a rare, but documented, side effect of this medication.

Second, he astutely discussed the ethical dilemmas he and his colleagues had encountered in performing the seminal

133

clinical trials of lithium's prophylactic effects during the 1960s, when there was increasing and even stinging criticism that this medication had never been subjected to a rigorous, double-blind, controlled investigation. Movingly, he reiterated his insistence that no clinical trial could be justified if it placed an untreated or placebo-treated patient at risk for suicide. He discussed the rationale for the elegant research design and statistical approaches he had used in his groundbreaking research, in which matched pairs of patients with bipolar disorder were formed, with one randomly assigned to placebo and the other to lithium. A given pair's trial was terminated at the first sign of clinical relapse of either member, minimizing risk of suicidal behavior to the greatest extent possible.[2] In addition, Schou had precalculated the numbers of pairs that would be needed to show significant benefits of active lithium, that is, which proportion of a given number of pairs would need to be placebo "failures" before a statistically significant result would emerge, ensuring that the trial would end as soon as clear-cut findings had been attained. Such dual concern for ethics and rigorous research methods was inspirational to me as an intern entering the mental health field

Schou also attended one of the support groups for patients with bipolar disorder that I co-led with another intern, Jay Wagener, a close friend and colleague of mine. This group had been a highlight of my internship year, with intensive discussions each week of symptoms, disrupted lives, and troubled histories as well as strategies for coping with the disorder. Occasionally, "breakthrough" episodes emerged during sessions, requiring immediate clinical attention. This clinical experience made a lasting impression on me regarding the utter need for psychosocial supports in the lives of persons with mood disorders, reinforcing the point that medications can work only if individuals are willing to take them. Group support and peer confrontation may be far more effective for many patients than one-on-one prodding from a professional in this regard.[3]

We asked the members of the group for permission to let Professor Schou sit in on a session. All had read at least some of his work on lithium, which we had suggested to them previously, and they readily agreed to his coming to the group. After listening attentively to the group process for most of the session, Schou finally spoke toward the end of the meeting. He told the members that, despite his clear belief in the efficacy of lithium and of the promise of newer medications yet to be discovered, his firm hope was that support groups could one day supplement or even supplant pharmacologic treatment, by providing an early warning system whereby patients could forecast incipient episodes in enough time to reinitiate treatments and thwart the new symptoms. These were strong words, indeed, on the potential value of psychological/social support treatments for bipolar disorder, coming as they did from the world's leading investigator of lithium.

The internship year consolidated my realization that I could integrate teaching, research on childhood psychopathology, and clinical intervention and supervision, three skills I had worked to hard to attain throughout graduate school, in an academic career. My rotation at the Affective Disorders Clinic also greatly enhanced my sense of connection with my father, fueling a growing realization that his story had important historical meaning, in the context of the many thousands of misdiagnosed individuals in the United States during much of the twentieth century. Once my internship ended, I eagerly finished my dissertation, which dealt with combinations of medication and self-management therapies for children with attention deficit disorder, within a few months.[4] My goal was to obtain a faculty position to continue such work. In the meantime, I obtained an initial postdoctoral position at the University of California, Irvine, and then a formal postdoctoral fellowship at the University of California, San Francisco.

In 1984, during the first spring of my postdoctoral fellowship in Northern California, my father experienced another "breakthrough" hypomanic episode once he and my mother returned to the Midwest following their Palm Springs stay. The episode was not severe enough to lead to hospitalization, but it was clearly of concern to my mother. I talked with her and with my father over the telephone, not helping much but hoping that the lithium would help to "shore up the dam" of any resistance he had to a full-blown episode.

During this period he produced a number of handwritten pages on legal pads, as well as typed documents, which he revealed to me a number of years later. These writings have been the source of some of the excerpts in this work. On one page he noted dreams that he had been having:

of Bertrand Russell...
of son Steve and of my boyhood home...
of an "anthropological," "archeological" investigation of the County hospital in Los Angeles [where he had been initially institutionalized at age 16]...
of a recent incident on September 6, which recalled the same date in 1936 when I jumped off the porch roof...

He had also looked up the term "grandiosity" in the glossary of the American Psychiatric Association's *Diagnostic and Statistical Manual of Mental Disorders*:[5]

...an inflated appraisal of one's worth, power, knowledge, importance, or identity. When extreme, may be of delusional proportions... e.g., a professor – who thinks, as lecturer, that he's God's gift to the students – but is, in reality, a crashing bore.

Perhaps he had begun to introspect about lectures he himself had given while in manic states, wondering to himself just how compelling a speaker he had actually been.

Other pages revealed additional experiences:

Recall also seance-like experiences in the classroom, during choir rehearsals and performances...where someone is decidedly in charge of the situation...for example, our choir...doing its best when they feel...dominated [by the director]. If their anger is stifled, and they direct their energies into singing better than before, they become conscious of the beauty of the music in ways they seldom have before. With religious themes being sung, the result is tears in the eyes...and feelings of mild ecstasy. There is a delicate balance of tensions here. Anger or frustration at being so dominated by the director's tendencies, and then masochistic feelings of pleasure or joy in being so dominated because one knows that only through such verbal punishment will he/she master the work being rehearsed or, later, being performed. We are chastised, and learn to "love" it as a necessary condition for becoming a good or great choir. Yet as we become better at singing the given Requiem, we may be overcome by its passages – tears (even sobbing) may momentarily make us mime rather than sing. There is now present a religious ecstasy, a kind of communicating with the Lord through the Spirit. Just as breath-takingly exhilarating experiences of Anza Borrego or of the Grand Tetons "reveal" the spiritual aspects of the universe, so do experiences of singing Verdi's Requiem.

He concluded this section:

One is surely handicapped in understanding human behavior and potentials of animals/higher animals if one has never been hypermanic [*sic*] over extended periods of time.

I sense in these words a continuing preoccupation with punishment and performance and with free will versus

137

authoritarian control. These "poles" had loomed large for my father since the time of his punitive experiences at the hands of his stepmother, over half a century before. I also see in his writing the expansiveness of thinking characteristic of hypomania, with freely flowing juxtapositions and the promise of religious ecstasy lying close underneath the surface of events such as the singing of hymns.

In yet another lined booklet, this one resembling a "blue book" used by college students for their final examinations, he wrote expansively in longhand, his flowing handwriting punctuated by arrows in the margins, leaving the impression of both free ranging emotions and crowded thought. The second sentence stands out:

The years of silence are past. . . .

The meaning is not entirely clear: a momentary, hypomanic thought? A sense of having finally disclosed his worst experiences, if only to himself in his many journal pages? Or to his son? A longing for intimate contact with someone who would understand him, forgive him?

At around this time, my father attended a talk at Ohio State given by R. D. Laing, whose writings he had admired and quoted for some time. Recall that it was Laing's *The Divided Self*, which I had given him as a Christmas gift fifteen years before, that spurred the conversations that he and I began to have. Following Laing's presentation, he introduced himself and invited "Ronnie" to the house after dinner. Laing accepted, and they talked and drank until very late in my father's study, sharing philosophical insights, experiences of psychosis, and religious themes. I can only imagine all of the subject matter that emerged that evening.

During my postdoctoral fellowship in the San Francisco Bay Area, I committed to my partner, and Roberta Wyn and I were married in the late summer of 1984. Our son Jeffrey was born in 1986. I had resolved any ambivalence about parenting long before he was born, and from the moment of his birth, I knew that fatherhood was a role I treasured.

At this time, I had accepted a visiting teaching appointment at the University of California, Berkeley, where I did my first independent teaching of undergraduate and graduate courses and where I continued with several research projects on which I had worked during my postdoc. During the spring of my year there, I was being considered for assistant professorships in psychology at both UCLA and UC Berkeley. The chairs of each department were in regular contact with me and with each other during the negotiation period. Each had inquired about my last name, asking whether I had a relative who taught philosophy at Ohio State. I told both of them that this was my father. As it turned out, each had been a student of his in the late 1940s, one as a graduate student (my father served on his dissertation committee) and the other as a returning undergraduate under the G.I. bill. They had both been entranced by his consultation and courses, which, they said, were intellectually rich and stimulating. When I told my father of this coincidence – that two of his former students were attempting to recruit me to their respective psychology departments – he told me that almost nothing he'd ever heard had filled him with such pride.

I decided to accept the job offer at UCLA and spent several productive years there in the late 1980s. UCLA's psychology department had just opened a new research center on children and childhood disorders, and I had a home for my research efforts. I was busy both as a new faculty member and a new father. Yet it was difficult being back in a faculty role at the department where I had been a graduate student just several years before. By the late 1980s, Berkeley had an opening for a tenure-track assistant professor in clinical psychology. After much indecision, I applied on the last day

139

possible, and subsequently received an invitation. I traveled back to Northern California for several days of interviews and colloquia to students and faculty, during a rainy week in late February. Things went well: My research was thriving, my record at UCLA was promising, and my prior teaching at Berkeley had been well received. I began to anticipate the thought of having the option to return to Berkeley. By the end of the summer, I had a formal job offer.

Deciding on the move was difficult. UCLA was now putting me up for tenure, to preempt my possible leaving for Berkeley; accepting the Berkeley offer would delay a tenure decision until I had taught there for a year or two, adding some risk to the decision. On the other hand, I felt that it would be better for my family to move back to Northern California.

Adding to the conflict was a subtle yet deep fear. Now approaching my late thirties, I was at the same phase in life at which my father had been in the latter part of the 1950s, following his numerous episodes of that decade. By that time, his career had already begun a slow, protracted decline. In part, I was asking myself whether I dared to surpass my father in terms of attainment. In blunt terms, how could I think of doing better academically than he? He was truly brilliant and creative, with a classical education, vast knowledge about esoteric realms of philosophy and the sciences, fluent in several languages. I am intelligent enough, my internal protest went on, thanks to my genes and the upbringing I received, but lack my father's incandescence. How could I ever measure up? And if I really did make the attempt, how fair would it be to have such an opportunity, when his had been taken from him?

I now believe that I was fearful of both outdoing my father and relinquishing the controlled way of working and living to which I had been clinging since childhood. Maybe it would be freeing to take the risk to work at Berkeley, yet the prospect was fraught with anxiety.

After much agonizing, I convinced myself that the move was worth it. We headed back to Berkeley in the fall of 1990. Within days, I realized that the choice had been the right one for me. The fears I had been harboring simply vanished: I felt freer intellectually than I had in years, ready for the challenge of working up to my potential. As I walked through the Berkeley campus during my early days on the faculty, I would remind myself each morning: "You're here! Make the most of it – what an opportunity!" I recalled, as well, that this was the campus to which my father had been awarded a full scholarship, worth $75, so many years before.

My inhibitions and fears that almost prevented the move had been fully my own. My father certainly wished that I attain as much as possible; I was the only one potentially putting the brakes on my accomplishments. Somehow I saw the wisdom of not succumbing to the safe route, the one that was dominated by survivor guilt, but the decision was far from simple.

The introduction to this chapter tells of my father's self-image as "a psychotic." As I described, this revelation floored me, flying in the face of my assumption that his diagnosis of bipolar disorder and his newfound knowledge of this condition would erase such self-perceptions. After all, I thought, here is a professor, a man of considerable intelligence, who has had the opportunity to benefit from readings, symposia, and consultations, all attesting to mounting evidence for the biological underpinnings of manic-depressive illness. Even though accurately diagnosed rather late in his life, why won't he or can't he "see the light"?

Upon reflection, however, I shouldn't have been so shocked at his words. During mid-adolescence, his world became completely unhinged, with a pernicious psychotic episode lasting many months and nearly costing his life. How could such

141

experiences, at age sixteen, have failed to alter his perceptions of himself and the world? In addition, the institutional settings in which he was housed and the fellow inmates who were his peers promoted a view of himself as out of control and deeply flawed, even deserving of punishment. He and his family received no education about mental disorder, given the field's pervasive ignorance and the lack of any semblance of follow-through or after-care. Once he had recovered from his initial episode as well as each one thereafter, he was basically on his own to resume his life. Even though his hallucinatory voices clearly abated during his euthymic periods, a different set of inner voices were always present to remind him of the depths to which he had sunk.

In retrospect, it would have actually been more shocking if his altered perceptions, punitive "treatments," and brutal environment during such a crucial period of identity formation had *not* had a profound and lasting impact on his core identity. Key experiences at such critical times as adolescence solidify belief systems (or "schema," to use a psychological term in common usage) that are not easily undone or discounted by recovery, book learning, or intellectual understanding. It may take only a minimum of reminders or triggers to activate such underlying perceptions, even during periods of normal mood and functioning. Set in motion are a host of prior beliefs and self-perceptions, which are not easily outweighed by attempts at reeducation.

For my father, simply reexperiencing in a cafe the types of individuals he had encountered in hospitals, whose thinking patterns and views of reality were markedly different from the norm, quickly uncovered his underlying identity as irrational, crazy, and psychotic. Perhaps he felt uniquely attuned to the struggles and emotional experiences of those people he heard in the cafe; perhaps, as well, he believed that only they or individuals like them could really understand the harrowing experiences he had undergone and the underlying identity at his core. The rest of the world could never know, given their insulation from such seminal life events.

Another theme pertinent to my father's self-image is the shame and dismay he experienced in relation to his history. He was a proud man, working hard to pull his life back together when his episodes had cleared. Yet privately, he was ashamed, puzzled by his experiences and their discontinuity with the rest of his life. Tellingly, his utter silence about his mental symptoms with almost everyone in his life bespoke the confusion and humiliation he felt inside.

Indeed, I recall vividly a poignant conversation with my father in his study in Columbus, during the last decade of his life. With a tender look on his face, he said that he had longed, for much of his lifetime, to have a physical illness to which he could attribute his episodes, anything tangible that he could pinpoint as a cause of his experiences, anything other than the feeling that it was all in his mind. "I'd have given almost anything to have had something that could be identified, that was real," he told me.

Part of the despair that surrounds mental illness is its inexplicability, its seeming emergence from one's core or soul, its view to the rest of the world as irrational and without any apparent cause or excuse except for one's weakness or flawed nature. Society's stance of distancing from people with such experiences and the utter lack of open discussion about mental disorder can serve only to perpetuate this sense of separation and aloneness as well as the conviction that persons suffering from mental illness must have selected or chosen to be this way or that they suffer from a fundamental moral flaw.

Even more, I have come to see that my father believed that he deserved the episodes he experienced, that they somehow must have been his own fault. Recall the earlier excerpts from his typed manuscripts, linking the punishments he received at the hands of his stepmother to the humiliation and degradation he experienced in mental hospitals. In a manuscript written later in his life, he invoked the concepts of Erving Goffman and R. D. Laing[6] in stating that ritualized punishment, early in life,

> ...may well be a milestone on the road to illness. In some weird sense it might be thought of as pertinent preparation for later commitment in which the son re-enacts his role as penitent, as "invalidated" human being. What formerly took a morning out of his day, now takes up to 5 months of his life. What formerly was momentary humiliation (of the protracted strapping that inevitably ensued), now takes months. What formerly was the first stage of the punishment ritual in which "guilt" was established by Mother, is now called a psychiatric examination or "degradation ceremonial"...wherein he is bereft of his civil liberties and, in effect, imprisoned in a total institution known as a mental hospital.

I see now that my father came to fear and expect punishment throughout his life, with mental hospitalizations now replacing the waiting, the spankings, and the humiliation he experienced as a boy. Despite his enhanced awareness, during the 1970s, of the psychobiological reality of his bipolar disorder, he still believed at some level that something he had thought, done, or failed to do – or perhaps some inner weakness – had led to a deserved and devastating set of punishments via hospitalization and ineffective, frightening treatments. Having any sense of control over bizarre and punitive experiences may be more reassuring than having no sense of control whatsoever, even if the cost of that perceived control is self-denigration and self-blame. Stated somewhat differently, it may be better to attribute lack of control and irrationality to one's own flaws and weaknesses than to contemplate a set of inexplicable, cruel, random processes at work. At least some control is maintained by so doing, even if the cost is one's sense of integrity and self-worth.

In all, the education about bipolar disorder that my father obtained in his last decades helped him to realize that there was some "reality" to his condition. But such objective knowledge could not fully replace years of subjective experience as "a psychotic," bolstered by hospitalizations and maltreatment. His academic learning was both too little and too late to overcome his fundamental, underlying self-identification as flawed, different, and deserving of punishment and humiliation.

Although knowledge of neurotransmitters, genetics, and biological predispositions may help to assuage the guilt and shame that all too often accompany serious mental illness, the tendency for self-blame is likely to be strongly present when the afflicted organ is one's brain.* In addition, the understandable desire to assert personal control over most of life's outcomes, so common in Western societies today, may seriously undermine self-esteem when the devastating consequences of mental illness are under consideration. The cost of assuming personal control and responsibility is to blame one's own weaknesses for mental disorganization and irrationality. One of the serious challenges ahead for both investigators

---

* In his compelling book, *A Mood Apart: Depression, Mania, and Other Afflictions of the Self* (New York: Basic Books, 1997), Peter Whybrow discusses such issues, taking the following stance:

> Depression and manic depression are thus very special diseases of the brain; they are afflictions of the private person – of the emotional self. It is not easy to recognize or accept their intruding presence, for in disturbing the neurobiological systems that regulate the *emotional* brain, they distort *person*ality. The difficulty in separating self from illness is a recurring confusion in mood disorder and lies at the root of much of the public stigma and misunderstanding.

of psychopathology and clinicians is to understand how the symptomatology and experience of mental disorder operate across various developmental phases and stages to foster self-awareness, self-understanding, and self-concept.[7]

From this perspective, it is a mistake to view mental disorders as fixed, static categories of interconnected symptoms. Rather, they are processes that organize and "pull" the individual's entire sense of being in various directions. Such directions are likely to be negative and self-denigrating when the individual is encountered by societies that fear, blame, and punish the experiences of mental illness and demand silence and distancing in their aftermath. The symptoms themselves leave their own scars on the individual, in the form of memories that are difficult to overcome and life events that cannot be undone. But if the attitudes of society about these symptoms and events become internalized and if they are interpreted as moral flaws or personal faults, deserving of silence and shame, the pain can only magnify.

Certainly, the field's vastly expanding scientific knowledge about mental disorders brings with it the real hope of far better treatment strategies and even of prevention. After centuries and millennia of nearly total ignorance, there is mounting cause for optimism. Yet rectifying our growing understanding of causes and mechanisms of mental illness with the intensely personal perspective of the individual who encounters its disorganization and terror is a continuing challenge. Increased knowledge of genes, neurotransmitters, and life events is essential, but there is still a large gap, even a chasm, between such knowledge and the individual's inner reality.

Indeed, making the link between scientific and personal perspectives and between objective and experiential frameworks is one of my key goals for the present work. Mental health research is still underfunded, mental health services are still fragmented, and the journey is still long for afflicted individuals and those close to them.[8] In comparison with the destructive power of mental disorder, our knowledge base is meager. I fervently hope that the best minds and most empathic hearts of future generations will be attracted to scientific and clinical roles in the field.

10

Final Years

It is March 1993, nighttime in Palm Springs, California. The sky is black velvet. The aquamarine swimming pool outside my parent's townhouse is framed by palm trees and stars. My father is here with my mother, but he is noticeably different this time. His gait is slow and halting, and he is at risk of losing his balance each time he walks. He has trouble reading complicated material: When reading novels, even simple ones, he must ask repeatedly about the plot. His quick smile and wit are replaced by a tight, frozen facial expression that betrays little emotion.

Still intact, however, is his long-term memory and his ability to converse about the past. I have begun to think of my father as having transformed into a kind of spirit, housed in a withering physical vessel, with increasingly limited abilities to process new information but with nearly full capability of reflecting on his history and his life.

The day has been a good one. My father is enjoying time with his six-year-old grandson, whose happy but volatile temperament reminds him of himself as a boy. My father and I have continued to talk about his life, in the moments available to do so. Now it is nighttime, and father and son again have time to themselves. The stars press down from the black sky above, as the air cools off after the day's heat.

Final Years

My father clearly wants to tell me something. We don't get far into our discussion before he says that he feels he has lived a wonderful life, full of rich encounters, full of interesting people, students he has taught, exciting ideas shared. "I wouldn't trade any of my experiences," he tells me. Even the psychotic periods were revealing, he says, if sometimes terrifying. His attitude is gentle, thoughtful, genuine, and philosophical in the richest sense of the word. He is at peace with himself and his life.

I marvel at his stance. Inside myself, I still feel frustrated over what has happened throughout his history, still angry with his doctors, still discouraged at the callousness of his treatments and the lack of motivation, it sometimes seems, on the part of those in the field to make fundamental changes in knowledge and attitude. How can he be so rectified to his fate?

It helps to recall that many whom I've met professionally and whose work I've encountered are eager for sound knowledge to replace ignorance and cavalier "care." But somehow, the anger and impatience I feel are hard to let go.

Still, it is my father's life, I remind myself, and he is the final judge of what has happened during its course. I admire his attitude of expansive forgiveness and peace. I wonder if I will ever feel the same way about my own life.

My father had been a regular smoker since late adolescence. As befitting a philosopher, he smoked pipes when reading or studying, first in college and throughout the time that I was a small child. He smoked cigarettes even more frequently thereafter. He decided to quit smoking altogether on my mother's birthday in May, 1989, a few months before he turned seventy. He did so, cold turkey, and told me several times afterward that he was proud that he had done so.

Within a few weeks, however, he began to experience problems with his voice. He had trouble maintaining its volume; his words sounded raspy and "thin" over the phone. He initially attributed this problem to throat irritations, but his physician's prescription of medicine for infections and allergies did nothing to alleviate the problem. When I would telephone him, his voice level faded markedly unless I prompted him to speak up, right into the receiver. Something was clearly wrong.

By the next year, his cognitive functioning had begun to decline more noticeably. He also began to display "freezing" of ongoing behavior, in which he would get stuck while standing up or while performing some other act, taking many seconds to get unstuck and continue with the action. He also began to develop a slow, shuffling gait while walking. His word-finding difficulties, subtle at first, became more pronounced. The decline of the previous years was gathering speed.*

Around this time, he was invited to speak at the prestigious Gordon Research Conferences, which take place each year in New England. The paper he prepared for the conference, entitled "The Dialectics of Control," reflected his expansive ideas, blending Aristotle, Plato, Hume, Marx and Engels, and R. D. Laing (among others) in a whirlwind of images. My mother attended the conferences with my father. Sadly, she noted that, in attempting to deliver this paper, he had terrible trouble sequencing his thoughts and actions and difficulty turning his pages of text, leading to a disorganized presentation.

---

* Although I would never advocate smoking, nicotinic receptors in the brain appear to play a role in (1) suppressing the motoric decline characteristic of disorders like Parkinson's and (2) temporarily reducing some psychotic symptoms (L. E. Adler et al., "Schizophrenia, Sensory Gating, and Nicotinic Receptors," *Schizophrenia Bulletin* 24 (1998): 189–202; E. K. Perry et al., "Nicotinic Receptor Abnormalities in Alzheimer's and Parkinson's Diseases," *Journal of Neurology, Neurosurgery, and Psychiatry* 50 (1987): 806–9). Activation of this receptor may therefore have therapeutic value. It is essential to understand the complex interplay of multiple neurotransmitter systems if we are to understand and combat the pernicious symptoms of neurological and mental disorders.

In the fall of 1991, my father and mother flew to the San Francisco Bay Area for my father's fiftieth college reunion at Stanford. My father looked perceptibly frailer: He was drawn, slightly blank in expression, and thinner than he had been in decades. His gait was now slowed and he was becoming less steady on his feet. Colleagues and friends remarked on his changed demeanor and reduced strength.

By this time he had also began to disclose even more intimate details of his life in our conversations. He had begun hugging me during greetings, as opposed to his usual, rather formal handshake. I knew, however, that his feelings toward me did not require a hug for expression.

In the summer of 1992, I made a visit back to Columbus with my son, then aged five and a half. My father and I took him to a playground, watching Jeffrey's active play on the swings and beams. "Grandpa" wanted to walk out on one of the climbing structures, to reexperience that kind of play, and asked me to walk with him in case his balance wasn't good. As he began to walk, however, he began to freeze, retreating back with ginger steps. He looked perplexed, then resigned. His motor problems were clearly becoming more severe, and I asked him what he was experiencing. "The 'fraids," he replied, explaining that he was becoming increasingly anxious, as he sometimes had been as a child, when he would claim that the 'fraids had taken hold of him. He was losing muscle mass, and his face was less and less expressive.

In December of 1992, I spent the initial days of the Christmas holiday in Berkeley writing an annotated outline of my father's life in preparation for his consultation with a senior neurologist at Ohio State. The problems he was facing in daily living had made it clear that he required such neurological examination. In as precise a fashion as I could, I documented the family history of mental disorder, my father's personal history of episodes, the range of treatments he had received, and the gradual decline in cognitive functioning that I had witnessed over the preceding years. I had been in the role of consultant and advice-giver before, but this time I had the distinct sense that it would be one of the final times I would do so.

Following the consultation, the neurologist gave a diagnosis of "Parkinson-plus" with strong suspicion of Lewy body dementia. This diagnosis signified a form of Parkinson's disease in which problems with "higher" cognitive functions (word consolidation, new learning) accompanied the motoric symptoms (slowing, rigidity, tremor) typical of Parkinson's.[1] My father was stunned with the diagnosis, and he began to read everything he could about the disorder. He was increasingly aware of his diminished skills and of his vulnerability. He stopped driving, graciously stating that he might not be quick enough to stop if he encountered a pedestrian, and had to terminate his singing in the church choir. Eventually, he curtailed his beloved activity of extensive reading, as he could not follow complex ideas or plots. He wasn't bitter, it seemed to me, but resigned, albeit with a real dignity.

In terms of treatment, the neurologist discontinued my father's lithium and started him on L-DOPA and deprenyl, two agents that facilitate neurotransmission of dopamine, in the hope of quelling the Parkinson's symptoms. My father's response to these agents, however, was disappointing. When Parkinson's is complex, accompanied by signs of dementia with Lewy bodies (named for the characteristic alterations in neurons found post-mortem), the usual treatments are often not very helpful.

During this time I began to consider the possibility of recounting my father's story. I was becoming more open emotionally, which was the key step toward recalling and reflecting on the importance of my father's experiences. Friends pushed me toward greater emotional give and take. Also, since the time of the internship rotation at the UCLA Affective Disorders

Clinic, I had increasingly realized that the story of his life reflected important historical trends in the field and might be instructive to others. Initially, my focus was on his longstanding misdiagnosis, with an emphasis on the need for accurate assessment and diagnosis. Yet his disclosures to me focused increasingly on his complex childhood and his stepmother's treatment of him, as well as his pervasive self-image as "a psychotic," adding layers of complexity to my understanding of his life. I realized that, in order to convey the full story, I would need to bring in these additional themes. Still, these were just ideas, with nothing yet committed to paper.

I began to talk in more depth with trusted friends and colleagues about my father's life and my potentially disclosing it. You must write, each of them encouraged me, both for yourself and for others to hear. Still, I hesitated. It's too private; I can't capture the essence of it on paper; it's safer to keep quiet in any event. I thus delayed any writing, wondering how I would be able to bring myself to begin the process.

In the spring of 1994, my father and mother returned again to Palm Springs in March. Up in Berkeley, I noticed an announcement for a conference on the history of science to be held later in the spring, featuring many intellectual issues that had been of central interest to my father throughout his life. I spoke with my mother and made arrangements for him to travel up for the conference in early May.

My mother and I discussed whether he could make the journey alone. Finally deciding that it was worth a try, she got him on a plane from Palm Springs to Oakland, where he sat, anxiously and rigidly, near the front, for the hour-long flight. Jeffrey and I greeted him at the gate, watching him slowly walk down the corridor to the arrival area. It took us many minutes to make our way through the terminal, slowly and unsteadily. At the escalator leading to the exit, he began to place his foot on the descending step but then froze, unsure as to how he could balance himself. He simply couldn't co-ordinate the placing of his feet on the moving stairs, fearful of falling. We slowly retreated to the elevator to go down one floor to the exit, with the crowds around us clearly annoyed by our slow pace.

We ordered in pizza that evening, and he was glad to be back in Berkeley. But it took him an agonizingly long time to unpack his suitcase, to eat dinner, and to get ready for bed.

The next day, at the conference, he greeted Berkeley and Stanford colleagues from past years, who were also attending this conference. Although he had trouble tracking all of the talks, he enjoyed the academic atmosphere. An old friend of mine, a fellow graduate student from UCLA days, with a keen mind and sharp wit, had come with us, sharing the day's conference. That afternoon, on the walk up to the Faculty Club following the last talk, he took a photograph of father and son, standing on the Berkeley campus near a famous "NL" parking sign, signifying a parking space reserved for Nobel Laureates.

As evening approached, the three of us sat on the patio of the Faculty Club, sipping drinks under the deep green of the trees and savoring the last of the day's golden sunlight. It was a priceless moment. I was infinitely grateful that my father could be with us on campus, sharing intellectual ideas. He and I had begun our talks about his life almost a quarter of a century earlier, and we were still able to commune in the type of academic setting that had been his lifelong home. At the same time, I realized that moments like this one would soon be impossible.

Not long into the after-dinner talk, my father began to drift off, unable to stay awake. We guided him across campus, in the darkness, to the parking lot to head home. It was the last academic conference that he ever attended.

The next academic year I took a sabbatical, which allowed me to initiate a large research project and also afforded me more time to travel. In September, I flew to Columbus for a short visit. It was early autumn in the Midwest, with warm, beautiful days and cool nights.

Outside in our backyard, sitting at a picnic bench on a warm afternoon, my father recounted the early September day, fifty-eight years earlier, on which he had jumped from the porch roof after walking through the streets much of the previous night. Although I had heard the story before, my father was more explicit than ever about his walk through the darkened streets, his approach to the house in the morning, and his conviction that his act could make a statement against fascism. It was clear to me that he was making his recollections more explicit than ever, pondering them ever more closely.

Several months later, in January 1995, I again traveled to the family home in Columbus and sat with him in his study on a snowy afternoon, amidst the warm wood tones and his extensive collection of books. The talk began as had so many others, with gentle questions and reflections. But soon it became clear that he had an agenda, as he stood to search for file folders that he eagerly wanted to show me. Walking with painstaking slowness to the filing cabinet, he opened the drawer and awkwardly fumbled through folder after folder, amidst the confusion of course syllabi, notes on ancient and modern philosophy, and departmental business that crowded his files. He struggled to stay organized and focused, his hands not readily able to perform the task of sorting through and opening folders. I tried not to be impatient, knowing that he was looking for something important.

Finally, he found the folder he had been seeking. In it were many of the handwritten and typewritten notes I have quoted in these pages, with information about his youth, his step-mother, his hospitalizations, and his insights. It was the first time that I had seen some of these writings, particularly the ones that probed his history most deeply. As his time was

155

running out, he was revealing to me his most important documents and most important secrets.

At the same time, my plans for writing about his life had begun to consolidate. I took the opportunity, amidst his showing me these papers, to ask him whether I could write about what he had been revealing to me over the years. I told him, slowly and explicitly, that I believed his story could be helpful to others. It was frustrating trying to communicate with him in this way, as he was still quite focused on showing me the folders and their contents. He was having trouble "shifting gears" to consider my question. Patiently, I pressed him, asking once more. This time he nodded, solemnly, understanding my request and assenting to it.

This was our last talk in his study. It is clear to me now that each of us had fulfilled his agenda that winter afternoon.

When my father came to Palm Springs with my mother several weeks later, in March, his behavior was more challenging and erratic than ever. Early in their stay, he threw a cup of water on a nightlight in the bedroom, convinced that flames were emerging from it. Such behavior is a sure sign of delirium, a mental state betraying serious deficits in consciousness, reasoning, and judgment. My mother didn't know what to do.

For a few weeks thereafter, he stabilized somewhat, getting into the daily routine in California and even appearing to improve cognitively. He tried walking, each day, around the grounds, to keep up his muscle tone, something that he hadn't been able to do for many months.

Yet by the time they arrived back in Columbus late in the spring, he had become increasingly incoherent. By late May, he was largely bedridden, even becoming incontinent. He had great difficulty lifting himself from his bed; my mother was not able to carry his dead weight to the bathroom. I urged her to get him to a hospital, and she clearly realized that he could not continue to stay at home.

I called my parents on June 12, their forty-fifth wedding anniversary. To my surprise, my father held his own during our brief phone conversation, though I knew that his physical abilities were by now sorely lacking. He attempted to joke, and he sounded comfortable.

Within the next ten days, and through great effort – in order not to frighten him with an ambulance and emergency medical technicians – my mother arranged for relatives and a friend to carry him to a waiting car to transport him to the local hospital. His condition was rapidly worsening: He was completely unable to walk unaided by this time. Although clearly at the end of her physical and emotional abilities to caretake him, my mother showed respect for his dignity to the last.

From a conference in New York at which I was speaking, I flew to Columbus in late June, rushing to the hospital to see my father. I did not know how alert or coherent he would be. He was gaunt in the hospital bed, but I was relieved that he at least recognized me, his face expressing joy at my arrival at his bedside. I was therefore initially encouraged. Yet when I left the room and returned a few minutes later, he was just as shocked and happy to see me as a few moments before. Clearly, and ominously, he was revealing severe problems with consolidation of new memories.

I desperately consulted with attending psychiatrists and neurologists. Is this a return of some form of bipolar disorder? Is this a worsening of his severe Parkinsonian condition? Regardless, it was evident that he was failing rapidly. The next day, my mother and I drove to several nursing homes, considering which one might be optimal for Dad. It was a sad task, but my mother and I approached it as a necessary step. I realized that it would be a long road back, if he were ever to regain much cognitive functioning.

I returned to California to oversee one of the summer research camps for children with attentional and behavioral problems that I directed. Within a few days, my mother secured a space in a good nursing facility, and my father was transferred there from the hospital.

Back in California, my summer work was, as always, engrossing, with clinical, research, and administrative challenges arising each day at the camp, amidst a large staff and a flurry of children. I figured that my father would rest comfortably in the nursing home for a long while and perhaps even regain some of his prior level of functioning. I knew that he was in serious trouble, but I hoped for some stability and peace. At least my mother did not have to contend with the physically and emotionally draining task of trying to attend to him at home, an impossible chore given his current state.

Two weeks later, however, my mother me called to say that my father had developed a fever, in the nursing home, following an infection. I called back to check on his status. Over the next few days, despite the antibiotic treatment he had been given, the fever was not clearing. My mother was greatly concerned, as was I.

On the morning of July 22, my mother called early to say that the end was near, as all his systems were failing. Tired from the week's work and from worry about my father, I called for a flight and reserved a seat for the afternoon. I called my sister from Denver, where I had a layover, and Sally reported that he was resting comfortably in his nursing home bed and that my nighttime arrival should be fine. I landed in Columbus after 11 p.m., losing two more hours to the time change. At the airport, my mother and sister greeted me, solemnly, telling me that Dad had died just an hour before. Sally had sat with him, watching him take his last breaths, as my mother had taken a short break to go home and shower. No one had realized at the time that the end was so near.

We drove straight to the nursing home, where I saw my father's body at about midnight. I had a feeling of unreality, looking at his rigid body but peaceful face. He had aged considerably over the last few years. His hair had been black until he was nearly seventy; it was not fully gray even now. Although I knew that he had not been of sound enough mind to talk coherently for some time, I wished that I could speak with him one more time. How glad I was, though, that we had largely completed our talks and that I had seen him several times in the past year, allowing him to disclose his most private writings and allowing me to secure his permission for writing about his life.

The next day, I helped my mother with arrangements for the funeral and memorial service. That afternoon, my mother, sister, and I saw his body for a final time in the open casket. Tears welled up inside; I wished for someone to comfort me.

The burial took place on the following day, Monday, on a hot, intensely sunny late July morning. A small group of friends and relatives had gathered at the family burial grounds. Prayers were spoken. I watched as the casket was lowered into the earth.

I flew back to California that night to be with Jeffrey and to continue directing the summer camp for the rest of the week, returning to Columbus four days later for the service of memory at the church, held on the following Saturday. Two of my father's three remaining brothers – Randall, the economist, and Paul, the singer – had also flown in for the service.

Several hundred people were in attendance: friends, university colleagues, family. It opened with an oboe solo, poignant and tender, followed by other classical music from a small group of Columbus Symphony players. Next were prayers and hymns, with the choir in front of the congregation, the choir with whom he had sung for over thirty years. Following words from the minister, Randall spoke warmly of his younger brother, Junior, recalling childhood memories, graduate school at Princeton, and more recent family visits and

159

reunions. Too emotional to sing at the service, Paul recalled the warm caretaking he received as a child from his older half-brother, including the sports they played together. He recalled that his brother had been Jackie Robinson's squad leader in junior high school.

I then spoke. Looking out at the assembled friends and family, I described my father's life. I noted his early years, the loss of his mother when he was three, the family's move to Pasadena. I spoke of his academic successes as well as his history of hospitalizations. My theme was that he had transcended his misdiagnosed bipolar disorder to develop as a teacher, philosopher, and loving father. I told the two stories of the number 100 – my kindergarten question about the populations of Russia and China, and my fourth-grade sleeplessness that was aided by my father's telling me I'd live to be 100 years old. I talked of my father's lifelong desire to look for the philosophical and spiritual underpinnings of the indescribable mysteries of everyday existence. I repeated a short quotation from Bertrand Russell, which my father had placed at the end of his own self-description for *Who's Who*. Nearly eighty years of age when he wrote it in *The Impact of Science on Society*, Russell was describing love or compassion:

> If you feel this, you have a motive for existence, a guide in action, a reason for courage, and an imperative necessity for intellectual honesty.

Finally, I noted my father's becoming more like a spirit as his body had faded in recent years but also stated that his spirit was still alive in me. As I spoke, I felt the same mixture of sadness, over the unrealized potential of my father's life; anger, at an ignorant mental health profession; and joy, at having been his son, that I have often since experienced when reflecting on his life and our relationship. I spoke with conviction, as many of these words had been waiting a long time to be said and heard in public. At the same time, I hoped that other people would read and hear these words, once I had written them all down.

After having dinner with my relatives, and after visiting the gravesite the next morning, I flew back to my life in California.

11

Causes and
Treatments

My father's life vividly illustrates key themes about the
causes and triggers of serious mental disturbance such
as bipolar disorder, and it raises central issues about both
treatment strategies and professional attitudes toward intervention. I therefore devote this chapter to these two themes.

Causal Factors

It would simplify matters greatly to state that my father's
bipolar disorder resulted exclusively from his genes. In fact,
investigations of behavioral genetics, which are based largely
on patterns of inheritance in twin and adoption studies,
have clearly demonstrated a strong genetic basis for bipolar
disorder.[1] First, identical (monozygotic) twins, who share 100
percent of their genetic material, have a far greater chance
of both having bipolar disorder than do fraternal (dizygotic)
twins, who, like any siblings, share on average only 50 percent
of their genes. In the language of genetics, the concordance
rate for monozygotic twins far exceeds that for dizygotic twins.
Second, studies of early-life adoptions demonstrate that the
risk for serious mood disorders congregates in the biological relatives rather than the adoptive relatives of those with

the disorders, even though these biological relatives never had contact with the adoptee beyond the first months of life. The effects for bipolar disorder are particularly noteworthy in this regard. In all, with the exception of single-gene disorders like Huntington's disease, bipolar disorder shows a pattern of inheritance as strong as that of any psychiatric disorder ever studied – for instance, its heritability is stronger than that for schizophrenia. The only conditions that appear to approach the figures for bipolar disorder are attention-deficit hyperactivity disorder and autistic disorder.[2]

Indeed, active searches are now under way at a molecular genetic level for the "bipolar gene" – or, more accurately, for the several different genes that may contribute to vulnerability for this condition. In the late 1980s, there was considerable excitement in the field, as a specific gene for bipolar disorder was thought to have been isolated in the Pennsylvania Amish population. Yet, upon further analyses of these data, the finding failed to replicate.[3] During the ensuing decade, other attempts to isolate a single gene responsible for bipolar disorder also proved unsuccessful.[4] The same state of affairs has pertained to other psychiatric disorders known to have substantial patterns of inheritance. In all probability, and unlike diseases like sickle cell anemia or Huntington's disease, no one gene is responsible for bipolar disorder. Rather, it may take the summation of several different genetic anomalies to yield strong risk for this condition. It is also possible that several distinct major genes are implicated in different forms of the disorder, all of which appear similar at the level of symptoms but which betray different sets of underlying genetic risk.

Using genetic terminology, influential investigators have contended that bipolar disorder is likely to be "oligogenic," meaning that multiple, small-effect genes interact with one another and with the environment to confer risk. In his vivid account of the search for "mood genes," Samuel Barondes emphatically points out that, as heritable as bipolar disorder is, the final story is highly likely to be complex rather than simple, with strong probability of the involvement of several specific genes as well as their interactions with the environment.[5] Although the recent unmasking of the human genome now gives the field a map from which to work, we should not count on single, simple genetic loci for most psychiatric illnesses. The same state of affairs applies to a host of complex medical conditions such as coronary artery disease, hypertension, and cancer, those diseases that confer the greatest mortality in developed nations.[6] Thus, even though it would simplify matters to contend that my father carried a single, aberrant gene that gave rise to his lifelong history of bipolar disorder, this simplification would undoubtedly be incorrect.

The concept of heritability is, in fact, quite often misunderstood. Heritability refers to the proportion or percentage of individual differences in the distribution of a given trait or disorder that are attributable to inborn, genetic causes as opposed to environmental influences. (Note that environmental influences may be shared across family members, like social class or general parenting style, or may be specific to individuals within a family – for example, unique parent-child interactions or the different patterns of peer relations for different siblings.) Taking height as an example, we might ask how much the considerable differences in adult height across a given population are related to genetic versus environmental influences. In point of fact, the heritability of ultimate height is quite high: At least 80 percent of the variation in heights is related to genetic differences between people rather than differences in their environments.

Three points immediately become salient. First, the term "heritability" does not apply to a given individual. Indeed, asking how much any one person's characteristics are related to genetic versus environmental causes is not a meaningful question. The answer is always "both," because all individual traits are determined by the interaction of the genotype with the environment, which creates the phenotype. My height, my intelligence, and my personality composition are entirely the products of both my genes *and* my experiences. Heritability, on the other hand, refers to genetic influences across a whole population.

Second, and closely related, a trait or disorder with strong heritability may still (at the level of the individual) yield to complex forces beyond the genetic level with respect to the expression of the trait or disorder. Gottlieb has made this point most forcefully in his critiques of "genetic dogma."[7] A striking example comes from recent work on cloning: "CC," the first cloned cat, has a pattern of fur coloring different from that of the cat from which she was cloned, signifying that factors beyond DNA composition influence this trait.

Third, there is no single gene for most complex characteristics, using height once again as an example. A person's ultimate stature depends on the interaction of a great many genes, acting in concert with one another and with environmental influences, such as diet and amount of sleep. Thus, a trait with strong heritability, such as height, does not automatically imply that the genetic picture will be simple.

Returning to bipolar disorder, the specific figures for its heritability approach those for height, with current estimates placed at 70 to 80 percent (or even higher). Thus, individual differences in the risk for developing manic-depressive cycles appear to reside largely in the genes with which individuals are born. Yet even for entities that are largely (or even exclusively) heritable, the environment may still strongly influence an individual's expression of the trait or disorder. For instance, the cause of a rare disorder called phenylketonuria (PKU) is inheritance of both alleles of a recessive gene that controls the body's ability to metabolize phenylalanine, a common amino acid. If

165

a person with the genotype for PKU (i.e., both recessive forms of the gene) ingests this substance, common in many foods, toxic levels build in the brain. During development, such a buildup alters the formation and functioning of key brain regions, with mental retardation the usual result. Because PKU is the product of this single recessive gene, *all* of the individual differences in PKU status are attributable to inherited characteristics. That is, its heritability is 100 percent.

An extremely effective preventive treatment for PKU, however, involves restricting the diet to avoid phenylalanine. This is why all infants are regularly screened for PKU shortly after birth through blood tests. If the test is positive, dietary restrictions are immediately enforced. Crucially, elimination of phenylalanine from the diet prevents the development of nearly all symptoms of PKU, and mental retardation does not occur. The crucial point is that even for a disorder with complete heritability, an environmental factor (in this case, diet) may contribute markedly to the individual's brain development and expression of symptoms. Similarly, despite the strongly heritable nature of height, food intake (or, more dramatically, receipt of growth hormone) can influence adult stature at the level of an individual case. Indeed, adult heights have risen by several inches over the past century, not because of any known changes in genes but because of environmental (dietary) influences across most of the population.

Another example pertains to measured intelligence, for which there is substantial heritability, perhaps as high as 60 percent. Even here, early environment may substantially affect a given person's later intellectual performance. A dramatic demonstration is found in a provocative investigation by Rutter and colleagues.[8] This research group studied a group of Romanian children, reared in the horribly deprived and abusive conditions of Romanian orphanages during Nicolae Ceausescu's reign as dictator in the 1980s. Nearly all such children placed in such orphanages have been found to suffer from cognitive delays, many of these severe. Following the deposition and execution of Ceausescu and the shocking exposure of the brutal conditions inside the orphanages, a number of these children were soon adopted into British homes. This situation allowed for a test of the malleability of children's intelligence in the face of early deprivation through a drastic improvement in the environment.

Crucially for the investigation, some children had spent only a few months in the orphanages before being removed, but others had been there for two or three years. The only factor that determined this length of stay was sheer chance, that is, the dates that the children had been born in relation to their placement into adoptive homes. The research team examined the adopted children, as well as a control group of British adoptees who had never been in orphanages, first at age four and then again at age six. The key finding was that the group of children placed into such stable homes during the first half year of life, thus spending only several months in the orphanages, showed nearly normal levels of intelligence by age four. Those for whom placement had only occurred after several years in an orphanage, however, showed compromised IQ scores during the preschool evaluation, dangerously close, on average, to the mentally retarded range.

In short, through this "experiment of nature," the investigators demonstrated the clear influence of early environment on the heritable trait of intellectual performance. Even though individual differences in cognitive abilities have a clear genetic component, early experience can still be greatly influential.

Returning once more to bipolar disorder: Despite the strong heritability of this condition, it is quite conceivable that environmental factors may predict the individual expression of such important features as its age of onset, content of its key symptoms, and lifelong patterns of cycling. Indeed, sophisticated causal models of bipolar illness have empha-sized interactions and transactions between the person and the environment in relation to the timing of episodes. Notable in this vein is the work of Post,[9] who hypothesizes the crucial role, in genetically vulnerable individuals, of stressful or traumatic life events in precipitating initial bipolar episodes. In his view, persons with the genetic propensity for bipolar disorder may require substantial levels of psychosocial or psychobiological stressors, such as loss events or even substance abuse, to pre-cipitate the initial manic or depressive episodes. It is as though the genetic predisposition takes a great deal of "push" from the environment before it becomes unleashed. Crucially, however, the initial episodes render the individual more likely to display episodes in the future, at closer time intervals and without the requirement for such noteworthy triggers to unleash the sub-sequent cycles. Through a process likened to the "kindling" of seizure disorders, in which seizures may become more spon-taneously generated over the years, subsequent manias and depressions may emerge later in life with considerably less environmental "push." In Post's model, then, life events may be crucial for uncovering the underlying, genetically based propensity for bipolar illness, a propensity which, once emer-gent, tends to become self-perpetuating.[10]

How might any of this technical discussion pertain to my father? As for an underlying genetic vulnerability, I have discussed our extensive family history of mood disorders, suicide, substance abuse, and eating disorders, along with schizophrenia-spectrum disorders from my step-grandmother's side of the family. This striking pattern suggests (but does not prove) some sort of genetic, heritable predispo-sition. As of yet, several candidate genes for bipolar disorder have been identified, but there is no clear-cut molecular model at present.[11] Remember, too, that the genetic risk (when identi-fied) is likely to be probabilistic, rather than certain, operating at the level of interacting genes that operate in concert with the environment to produce vulnerability. Thus, what is likely to be inherited is a susceptibility to mood aberrations rather than a disease state per se.

If what my father inherited was a vulnerability rather than a certainty, what life experiences may have activated his underlying genetic risk? Certainly, the loss of his mother at age three must be considered. Some years ago, researchers and clinicians contended that early parental death was a major trigger for mood disorders. More recently, however, the role of early separation and loss in predisposing to mood disturbance has become the subject of considerable debate, with evidence both supporting and rejecting this hypothesis.[12] In my father's case, it is plausible that the loss of his mother during his early development interacted with his putative genetic predisposition to make him susceptible to mood disturbance, perhaps through a vulnerability to later loss events.

Next, from any perspective, including the sheer volume of my father's writings about the topic, his treatment at the hands of his stepmother was a key factor in his development. On the one hand, there is no compelling evidence for the contention that such abusive childrearing practices as those he experienced are specific causal factors in the development of bipolar disorder. On the other, the parenting he received profoundly shaped his self-image, influencing the ways in which he later interpreted many life events, including his hospitalizations. A large part of him believed that he was to blame for his episodes and punitive treatments, perhaps related to some moral weakness. Indeed, he seems to have been awaiting and anticipating punitive consequences throughout his life.

But what of the claim that the abuse experiences alone could have facilitated his development of bipolar disorder? Knowledgeable clinicians with whom I have discussed my father, particularly those holding to psychodynamic or family

systems perspectives, have commented on the potential ramifications of my step-grandmother's parenting style, which
blended abusive, sexualized discipline with soothing and mas-
saging "compensation" following her harshest punishments.
In this view, such reparation took away any chance my father
might have had to become angry or outraged, forcing a "solu-
tion" of subsequent identity loss and even psychosis.

It is difficult for me to accept such an extreme psychological and environmentalist position, largely because of the con-
clusive evidence for the strong heritability of bipolar disorder. In addition, current scholarship regarding physical and
sexual abuse does not suggest that it inevitably leads to any
distinct syndrome of behavioral and emotional reactions, and
certainly not to bipolar disorder per se. Rather, it portends
core conflicts – for example, lack of trust, boundary issues, and
betrayal – that interact with other individual and family characteristics to shape an individual's ultimate outcome.[13] I note,
however, that in a recent review, Post and colleagues conclude
that patients with bipolar disorder who also have histories of
physical or sexual abuse display a more pernicious course of
their manic-depressive illness, suggesting strongly that abuse
experiences interact with the underlying genetic risk to yield
a more severe form of the disorder.[14]

Overall, it is not possible to disentangle the complex web
of (1) family history of psychiatric disorder, (2) early loss
of his mother, and (c) abusive treatment during childhood
in explaining my father's developmental course. The models
that eventually emerge from sound research are likely to be
complex and transactional rather than straightforward and
linear.

In academic circles, there is renewed debate about the role
of important life events in activating underlying vulnerabilities, precipitating episodes, and influencing recovery patterns for persons with bipolar disorder.[15] In terms of onset

of episodes, Malkoff-Schwartz et al. have provocatively argued that key triggers for bipolar disorder are those types of stressful events that tend to disrupt daily routines or sleep-wake cycles, given the complex interplay between circadian rhythms and light/dark cycles, on the one hand, and risk for bipolar episodes, on the other. In other words, disrupted sleep is seen as a potential trigger for the onset of episodes in persons with the genetic vulnerability, as the rhythms involved in sleep are closely tied to those that may trigger mood disturbance.[16] Other types of life experiences may be pertinent for recovery from episodes. Specifically, negative life events are related to the length of time a person with bipolar disorder takes to regain euthymic functioning once an episode has begun.[17]

Progress in the field is most likely to emerge when scientists vacate positions of extreme biological or environmental reductionism and consider the complex interplay of biological and psychological causal factors that are likely to be involved in bipolar disorder as well as other major psychiatric conditions.[18] The ensuing models are not likely to be simple, but they are bound to be more accurate.

What types of life events appear to have been influential with respect to my father? Of course, hindsight may be 20/20, so I consider the following ideas as hypotheses at best. For one thing, losses (breaking up with a girlfriend) or events that could be interpreted as signifying loss (completion of his doctoral thesis) coincided with his 1945 episode. Similarly, the awarding of full professorship, coupled with our family's move to a new home, directly preceded his year-long episode and hospitalization in 1960–61, when I was in third grade. These latter events were not so much losses as major life transitions, which may have overloaded my father's "balance." In a vivid portrayal, Whybrow emphasizes the key role of disrupted attachments and loss of close contacts in triggering episodes for persons with vulnerabilities to mood disorders.[19]

In addition, my mother's pregnancies were salient triggers for two of my father's episodes, one a hypomanic episode during my mother's pregnancy with me, and the other a devastating, psychotic-level, full manic episode during her pregnancy with my sister. Research evidence exists, in fact, that childbirth is a correlate or instigator of manic episodes in both men and women with vulnerability to bipolar disorder.[20] What mechanisms might underlie this fascinating association in men? Is it the change in role to fatherhood? Or perhaps the potential "loss" of their partners to the ensuing parenting roles? The change in daily routine and sleep/wake cycles? A kind of existential fear of creating new life? Or some combination of the above? Much remains to be learned about such intriguing possibilities.

Consistent with Post's notion that manic and depressed episodes may become self-initiating and progressively more frequent across the lifespan, I point out that my father's initial, severe episodes at age sixteen and twenty-five gave way to a series of devastating, repeated cycles in the 1950s. The initial episodes of that decade may have been triggered by my mother's pregnancies, but they then seem to have emerged more spontaneously, without clear life stressors or other triggers. But then, following his lengthy episode and hospitalization from 1960 to 1961, and well before he began to receive lithium in the mid-1970s, the frequency and intensity of his cycles began to diminish. I have no compelling explanation for this pattern. Indeed, the life courses of most individuals with bipolar disorder do not fit into neat categorizations. We know today that persons with this disorder include those who display quite rapid cycles, ranging from hours to days, those whose episodes are regular and seasonal, and those with rather infrequent cycles that may require major life events as instigating factors. Causal theories of this disorder will have to contend with such strong individual variability.

Finally, I return to my earlier comment on Kraepelin's contention that individuals with manic-depressive illness typically return to normal levels of functioning between episodes. At first glance, this depiction appears to fit my father's life, as he showed a remarkable ability to recoup his losses and regain his "baseline" levels of functioning following his initial episodes. Indeed, some of his recoveries were as dramatic as the episodes themselves: his completion of twelfth grade with an A average in the spring of 1937, after his nearly fatal initial episode, and his attaining of an academic job following his protracted episode of 1945. At a personal level, I think of his sensitivity as a father in the years after his total absence from the family home in 1960–61.

But the depiction of mood disorders as encompassing complete recovery between cycles may be more mythical than real. Particularly as a history of episodes progresses, residual deficits in memory and cognitive functioning may accrue, even during euthymic periods.[21] My father, in fact, had begun a gradual decline in overall functioning by his late thirties, even during periods when he was not symptomatic. In between episodes, he displayed memory problems, poor regulation of arousal, and decreased motivation. Although these problems were subtle at first, they clearly intensified during the latter decades of his life, presaging the precipitous decline of his final years. Whereas the misguided treatments he was receiving may have played a role, it is increasingly recognized that bipolar disorder may take a cumulative, lifetime toll.[22]

In all, the psychological, psychosocial, and even neurobiological[23] ramifications of severe manias and depressions appear to be progressive and debilitating, and such effects will clearly be compounded if outdated or harmful treatments are used. Furthermore, even if euthymia does bring on a complete or nearly complete return of premorbid abilities, as may be the case following an individual's initial episodes, repairing broken relationships or dealing with the aftereffects of aberrant, impulsive behavior is bound to take a toll on self-esteem and self-image as well as on employment and family life. Whatever the combination of genetic and psychosocial causal factors involved in instigating bipolar episodes, clinicians must be cognizant of the devastation to individuals' lives as a result of severe mental illness and the shaping of underlying self-conceptions related to histories of repeated episodes.

Treatment and Care

Authoritative guides for treating patients with bipolar disorder now exist, as exemplified by the American Psychiatric Association's Practice Guidelines.[24] In brief, although antipsychotic medications may be necessary for initial symptom control during agitated periods of psychosis, medications such as lithium, carbamazepine, and divalproex are the mainstays of treatment for bipolar disorder, showing far greater efficacy than antipsychotic agents in controlling manias and, most clearly in the case of lithium, in regulating, diminishing, or even preventing subsequent manic and depressive episodes.[25] The use of these mood-stabilizing medications has been shown to prevent the self-destructive and suicidal behaviors that are so frequently associated with severe mood disorders.[26]

In some cases, these mood-stabilizing medications show an almost "night and day" effect, smoothing a roller-coaster life course to a regulated and protracted period of euthymia. More often, however, they serve to reduce the intensity and frequency of manic and depressed cycles and to lengthen the period of euthymia between episodes, without eliminating the mood swings altogether. Thus, in most cases they are not complete cures. The patient must be vigilant for "breakthrough" manias or depressions, which may well require an intensification of treatment.

Crucially, medications for bipolar disorder must be taken regularly if they are to exert beneficial effects.[27] As a result, the official guidelines and authoritative reviews also recognize the beneficial role of psychoeducation and structured psychotherapies to support medication adherence.[28] Noncompliance with medication treatment is, in fact, a major problem with respect to manic-depressive illness, for such reasons as denial, the desire on the part of patients to recapture the euphoria of hypomanic mood states, and the wish to avoid medication-related side effects.[29] Psychological treatments such as structured, professionally led support groups or psychoeducation about bipolar disorder may therefore be a necessary adjunct to pharmacologic intervention.[30] In addition, family-based treatments for persons with bipolar disorder have been shown to increase positive family interactions and improve patients' symptom trajectories over lengthy periods of time.[31]

Overall, the improved diagnostic criteria and the establishment of validated treatment regimens within the past several decades appear to signal a world completely different from that of my father's early years, with its almost total lack of knowledge about the diagnosis and treatment of severe psychopathology. He was warehoused for months at a time in hospitals that lacked even rudimentary treatments. Being an inmate of such "total institutions"[32] forged fundamental alterations in his identity, including his lifelong self-identification as "a psychotic," out of control and on a different plane of existence from most of the rest of humanity. And, as I have pointed out, his early childrearing experiences led him to consider such punitive treatment as deserved, inevitable, and even just. In contrast, the growth of knowledge about such severe mental illnesses as bipolar disorder has been meteoric in recent years, and the advent of mood-stabilizing medications like lithium has made the hope of normal functioning a reality for millions of individuals worldwide.

Despite the field's recent advances, however, the situation today is far from ideal, for a number of reasons.

(1) Far too many individuals with severe mental illness never receive access to mental health care at all.[33] In fact, the majority of people with mood disorders or other major psychopathology never receive adequate assessment or treatment, because of both reticence on their part to seek it and the lack of access to services for those who do. It is a cruel paradox that, despite the ever-increasing sophistication of our scientific understanding, access to empirically supported treatments remains dismally low.

(2) Public attitudes toward aberrant behavior and mental disorder have not uniformly improved. Indeed, stereotyping and stigmatization of irrational, psychotic behavior are still rampant.[34] Such stigma is perhaps the key issue underlying the lack of availability of appropriate treatment and care. Mental disorder is still attributed to blameworthy weakness, fundamental defects, or less-than-human qualities. Job discrimination, lack of housing, poorly coordinated policies, unrelenting self-blame, and family distress and silence continue as the norm for far too many individuals and families. And, lest we forget, exclusion from society and even genocide comprise much of the legacy of societal reactions to mental disorder.[35] Reduction of stigma is essential, as nearly all attendant issues in the field – funding, research, access to care, public commitment to change – emanate from basic attitudes that surround mental disorder.[36]

Along this line, one might legitimately ask why stigmatization of mental disorder still exists. After all, haven't our recent advances in scientific knowledge shown at least some forms of mental disorder to be as "real," or as genetically based, as many physical illnesses? And haven't our modern conceptions of abnormal behavior replaced prior perspectives, for example, that such behavior was a sign of possession by evil spirits or the devil, exemplifying demonology? Shouldn't society therefore stop making attributions to an afflicted individual's moral flaws, fundamental weakness, or lack of willpower? In reality, the situation is not so clear-cut. Attributing psychopathology to mental disorder rather than demonology or evil tendencies does not automatically eliminate blame and aspersion. As I have written elsewhere, with Dante Cicchetti:

> ...although attribution theory tells us that ascription of disordered behavior and emotion to illness (a non-controllable cause) should theoretically lead to more benign appraisals and consequences, the label of mental disorder or mental illness can indeed be accompanied by anger, punitive reactions, and exclusionary "treatment." ... Clearly, mentally disturbed behavior is still viewed as far more controllable than so-called physical illnesses; when the behavior in question is particularly frightening or noxious, fear appears to overtake more humane social reactions. The afflicted person may come to be blamed for susceptibility to having become "ill," especially given that the symptoms of the illness are disturbed emotions and behavior patterns, over which people are typically held to exert control. Note, then, an intriguing parallel between demonologic and medical-model perspectives: Both attribute abnormal behavior to non-controllable causes (i.e., demonic influence or mental illness), with the potential for increasing sympathy toward and reducing blame of the afflicted individual. Yet both also have led to extremely harsh, punitive reactions and interventions, because of fear, the tendency to blame the person for susceptibility to either "possession" by spirits or illness, and the typical perception that behavior and emotion should be controllable and controlled.[37]

In short, the modern tendency to ascribe aberrant behavior patterns to "mental illness" does not automatically eliminate stigma or promote social acceptance.

(3) Early detection of manic-depressive illness, before psychotic-proportion episodes have wreaked their havoc, is not yet a reality. Our ability to predict risk for severe mood disorders during childhood, or to recognize the presence of early-onset bipolar disorder in children, is far from perfect.[38] As a result, if treatments do get recommended and implemented for those with the disorder, they typically follow from the devastation that has already occurred.

(4) Current crises in medical and mental health insurance have cut hospital stays in psychiatric facilities to absurdly short time periods – a few days, in many cases. Despite the dangers of inhumane, inappropriate hospitalization, responsive hospital care may still be necessary for management of acute episodes. Yet establishing a medication regimen or initiating meaningful therapy cannot take place in such pitifully short intervals. Far too many individuals are released to inadequate care in the community well before medication regimens have been initiated, much less stabilized. And the lack of appropriate community care is currently at a crisis level, with a nearly total lack of adequacy of the kinds of supports (medication monitoring, support groups, employment training, and the like) that are needed by most individuals with severe thought disorders or mood disorders.

(5) Training in proper assessment and diagnosis is far from uniform across settings and professional disciplines. In fact, most treatment for psychopathology emanates from nonspecialists who lack any kind of training in appropriate diagnosis and intervention strategies.

(6) Complexities of real-world cases have led to a sobering reconsideration of the actual success rates of pharmacologic interventions for mood disorders. For example, manic-depressive illness is frequently clouded by troubling associated features (e.g., severely dysfunctional families, in some cases) as well as comorbid conditions (i.e., additional psychiatric

178

problems or conditions, such as serious substance abuse). These sobering problems and complications hamper accurate diagnosis, limit access to beneficial treatments, and seriously undermine compliance with such interventions even if they are obtained and funded. In fact, outside the rarefied atmosphere of highly selective clinical trials, benefits of lithium and other medications for bipolar disorder are not uniformly positive for many of the complex patients in the real world.[39]

In all, despite gratifying progress, intervention efforts have a long way to go before the field can even consider resting on its laurels. With the rapid advances that are now occurring in neurochemistry and molecular genetics, even more specific pharmacologic agents may well be developed in the near future, including those with fewer side effects and those that may be given preventively as individuals enter the risk period for episodes (e.g., adolescence). If such truly preventive agents are ever to be used effectively, however, accuracy of assessment and prediction must improve, so that individuals are not falsely labeled as "at risk" and subjected to unneeded treatments.

I wondered earlier whether my father's decline in his latter decades might be attributable not only to the cumulative toll of his repeated episodes but also to his years of receiving unnecessary neuroleptic medications, sleeping pills, and numerous electroconvulsive treatments. With regard to the latter, newer advances in ECT such as shorter pulses of current, adequate anesthesia, or delivery to only one hemisphere were not standard at the time that my father received this form of intervention.[40] In consulting with expert neurologists, psychiatrists, and psychologists about the possibility that neuroleptic treatment and numerous ECT sessions facilitated the complex Parkinson-like illness from which my father suffered in his last years, I have received wide-ranging opinions, from those that discount any possible link to those that acknowledge

179

their possible role.* I must point out that ECT is an extremely important and valuable treatment for many individuals with severe mood disorders who do not respond optimally to medication treatments.[41] Yet the key questions regarding my father are whether he would have needed it at all, had lithium been available earlier in the United States, and whether safer use of ECT might have precluded his development of side effects. In all, had appropriate treatment been available for my father, his time spent in severely disordered states could have been greatly diminished, reducing the risk to later cognitive functioning both from the episodes themselves and from misguided treatments.

A related point pertains to the way in which medications are approved for use by the Food and Drug Administration in the United States. The rigorous clinical trials that serve as the final round for ascertaining the safety and efficacy of new medications, termed Phase III trials, span weeks, not months or years. The upshot is that the field has essentially no long-term data about any new psychotropic medications as they are approved and released for use. Thus, we may simply not be certain about the long-term consequences of important medications until they have been used for many years in clinical settings. Clinicians must therefore strike a balance between appropriately aggressive intervention and needed caution, a balance not always easy to attain.

In closing, I raise several additional issues for professionals in the field. One, noted above, is that even with effective treatments, the patient's world view and self-image may have been substantially altered by prior episodes, disorganization, and psychosis, as well as by hospitalization experiences. Relatedly,

---

* Although Parkinson's appears to run in some families, the only case known among my father's relatives is that of his cousin – the man whom I met, as a boy, in Southern California, for whom L-DOPA provided initially dramatic improvement.

repairs may be needed in relationships, work settings, and bank accounts, even when effective treatments are applied. Stabilized mood via medication cannot, in and of itself, address such crucial social and psychological issues and such devastating sequelae of past episodes.

Furthermore, the patient's acceptance of a newly obtained diagnosis may be tenuous, and treatments may not be received with gratitude or with full (or even moderate) adherence. Being labeled as mentally disordered is not easy for many individuals to tolerate, given the pervasive effects of stigma in society, even though some patients may welcome the "reality" of knowing that their aberrant behavior has a certifiable, documented cause. As noted above, support groups are a potentially vital component of a total treatment package, for such diverse reasons as facilitating the "facing" of diagnosis, providing needed psychoeducation and social support, and motivating regular adherence to treatment. It may be far easier for a newly diagnosed individual to hear such messages from peers than from even the best intentioned and most skilled professional.

In addition, family members can and must be involved directly in the evaluation process as well as in the delivery of treatment. As discussed earlier, obtaining information about a patient's history or about the course of the current episode virtually requires the perspective of persons other than the patient himself or herself. And because insight is not uniformly strong in mania or depression, noncompliance with treatment or even active thwarting of therapeutic efforts is an unfortunate reality in too many cases.

Note that family members include the patient's children. Counter to the absolute prohibition that my father received from his psychiatrist regarding the provision of any information to my sister and me about his absences, clinicians and investigators realize today that speaking directly to children is vital to parent and offspring alike. Psychiatrist William

Beardslee of Harvard, for example, has pioneered a specific intervention for families in which a parent has significant depression. In this family-based treatment, one key task is for the parents to work toward constructing a collaborative narrative with the child, explaining the parent's depression in terms that are both familiar and understandable to the child or adolescent. These attempts to talk directly with the child, in order to prevent denial, unanswered questions, and the child's understandable tendency for self-blame, have shown real promise in improving children's psychosocial functioning and, more impressively, in diminishing their own risk for the emergence of depression in adolescence.[42]

Finally, professionals need to examine their own values and biases, including the deeply ingrained tendencies to view themselves as "us" and patients as "them." To the extent that individuals with mental disorders are viewed, unconsciously or consciously, as defective or subhuman, treatment will focus on isolative, punitive, and exclusionary models.[43] Interventions that fail to consider education and support of the patient as well as family members, that do not promote gains in the patient's everyday world, and that neglect the reality (despite their irrationality) of disturbed or psychotic experiences to patients themselves, are doomed to be both fragmented and nonresponsive to the complex web of expectancies, attributions, and personal relationships in which both healthy and disturbed functioning are embedded.

Today's and tomorrow's practitioners must continue to receive first-rate education and training in two parallel but ultimately converging areas: (1) the ever-expanding scientific knowledge base regarding assessment, diagnosis, underlying mechanisms of disorder, and treatment strategies; and (2) communication, understanding, and human compassion regarding contact with patients and families. Blending these two vital elements is a continuing challenge, but one that the mental health professions must actively embrace. Neither component alone is sufficient; both are required.

What initial steps might be taken in this regard? I make the following suggestions: better selection of those desiring to become workers in the field; stronger exposure to real-life ethical issues in the training of both clinicians and investigators; far greater integration of basic and applied scientific efforts, in order that the best scientific knowledge can dovetail with prevention and treatment efforts;[44] higher levels of recognition of the essential humanity of those individuals who suffer from extremes of irrationality and psychosis; and greater inclusion of the family in key assessment-related and treatment decisions. This is a partial list, but each point may constitute at least a small step.

Indeed, the stakes are bound to get higher, rather than lower, as more powerful and specific treatment strategies are discovered and as the potential for early (and even prenatal) recognition of major risk for serious mental disorder becomes a reality. Genetic medicine, genetic screening, and early prevention efforts all place a premium on greater, rather than lesser, attention to key ethical and clinical issues in the mental health professions. Among the crucial questions the field will face are the following: Will emphasis on prevention lead to routine genograms for unborn children, which specify percentages of risk for major mental disorders? Will there be a groundswell of support for aborting fetuses found to carry rates of such risk deemed unacceptably high? What will be the cost to society – and, indeed, to the entire human gene pool – if genetic risk factors for bipolar disorder are systematically eliminated? Will the increased perception of bipolar disorder as a condition with high heritability lead to a reduction in stigmatization or, more ominously, to increased perceptions of vulnerable individuals as genetically and biologically flawed or deviant? Will sufficient resources be allocated for the training and supervision of adequate numbers of clinicians to learn both sound scientific knowledge and nonexclusionary attitudes?

Only one future direction seems certain amidst such questions: The scientific and clinical challenges and the moral and ethical issues will not get any simpler in the coming years but will only grow in complexity. Are we as a field and we as a society ready?

12

Resilience and Social Context

In this chapter I take up two key questions. First, how can my father's positive attitude toward life – his satisfied sense in his last years that he wouldn't have traded any of his life's experiences – be reconciled with his history of episodes and maltreatment? In other words, what might explain his resilient attitude? And second, how did his intensely personal experiences of mania, depression, and psychosis reflect larger forces in the world? That is, how do inner and outer worlds coexist and blend together in the context of serious mental disturbance?

Resilience

Many individuals grow up in high-risk environments, plagued, for example, by poverty, abuse, absent parents, or caregivers with mental disorder. Others suffer from inborn problems, such as congenital defects or sensory losses like blindness or deafness. Still other individuals experience clear adversity during their lives, including traumatic life events, major bereavement, chronic physical illness, or mental disturbance. Although such risks, conditions, and experiences certainly increase the odds for negative outcomes and difficult life adjustment, some persons appear to overcome these odds[1]

185

by displaying unexpected coping abilities and strengths. My father's experience clearly shows that, in the face of severe mental disorder, despair and fragmentation are not inevitable.

Resilience is defined as the set of processes leading to positive outcomes within the context of significant risk or adversity.[2] For individuals to be resilient, there must, by definition, be exposure to adverse circumstances or extremely difficult life events, coupled with positive adaptation in the face of such risk. The scientific and clinical task is to discover those factors within the individual, within the family, and within the larger social context that facilitate such unexpectedly positive outcomes.

What risks did my father experience? Among salient factors, I can point to the loss of his mother at age three, his experience of abusive childhood punishments, and his having spent his late childhood and early adolescence during the height of the Great Depression. The most critical experience, however, is his initial episode at age sixteen, followed by half a year of being warehoused in a county facility, along with his history of bipolar disorder throughout the rest of his life. He therefore experienced several early "risk factors" as well as the devastation of suffering from a recurrent mental disorder.

A growing scientific literature documents that individuals at high risk, including victims of abuse as well as persons with serious mental disorder (plus their offspring), can function in resilient fashion.[3] Yet much remains to be learned about the developmental processes that facilitate such adaptation, hardiness, or transcendence. In terms of mental illness, not only do many persons with mental disorder have periods of remission, which are clearly characteristic of the cyclic course of mood disorders, but an appreciable number also manage to function in an adaptive fashion for prolonged periods of their lives despite having experienced the disorganizing, terrifying, and demoralizing symptoms of the disorder. The key question is how this subgroup achieves such an outcome.

In particular, how did my father pick up the pieces from his psychotic-level experiences and maltreatment and then proceed with his life, once his mind was clear following episodes? With what personal traits and through what processes did he maintain his ultimate self-acceptance? What did he believe, feel, and do to maintain and nurture such a perspective? Although the field has continued to learn more about the causes of and treatments for devastating psychopathologies, there has been a relative neglect of the study of positive attributes that may help to protect individuals from the negative outcomes that so often result from the extreme stress and adversity of mental disorder. Indeed, clinical psychology, psychiatry, and related disciplines have been dominated by investigations of negative events and negative outcomes at the expense of positive emotions and uplifting behaviors.[4] Perhaps something fundamental is being missed by such a predominant focus on pathology rather than health, despair rather than coping, and maladaptation rather than adaptation.*

---

* In some ways the criticism of the exclusive focus of the mental health professions on "psychopathology" is unfair. After all, the subject matter of psychiatry and clinical psychology is not healthy development and functioning but, by definition, atypical development and maladjustment. As a supervisor at UCLA once noted to my class, what would you think of an automobile mechanic who focused, in his appraisal, of what's working well with your car rather than what's wrong? In other words, there is a danger that neglecting the harsh realities of serious mental disorder by searching for positive features and characteristics could be Pollyanna-ish and ill-advised, not to mention neglectful.

Yet there are counterarguments to this position. For one thing, our very definitions of abnormal behavior or psychopathology are still quite incomplete, as the field is still seeking key knowledge about basic brain functioning, the interface between cognition and emotion, the development of self-regulation, and the like. In the absence of full information about basic, adaptive processes, our branding of certain behavioral and emotional patterns as "deviant" may well be premature. In addition, the range of outcomes for persons afflicted by any given category of mental disorder is so great that it is crucial to investigate and identify the mechanisms

At one level, resilience includes those personal characteristics, those inner "essences," that may facilitate positive outcome. A sense of humor, strong intelligence, a flexible temperament – such are the individual features that have been shown to predict resilient functioning.[5] Other factors contributing to "positive psychology" in general include the attributes of optimism, faith, interpersonal skill, courage, future-mindedness, strong work ethic, hope, and honesty.[6]

What of my father? Certainly, his work ethic and native intelligence played key roles during his entire life and particularly during periods of recovery. Yet these qualities alone do not seem sufficient to explain his resilience, as many intelligent, hard-working people do not appear to rebound from extenuating life circumstances. I think, rather, of his courage, tenacity, and religious faith. In addition, I would also point out his great tendency toward denial. The latter is a double-edged sword. As painful as silence and denial can be, there may be some real adaptive value to shutting out the worst of one's behavior as well as the consequences of one's severely psychopathological states. Indeed, after severe manic or psychotic states there may be a kind of merciful amnesia for the worst devastation of the episode – although workmates, partners, and family members may not be blessed with a parallel amnesia. In my father's case, his ability to forget, at least temporarily, what he had just been through and to focus on the present may have been beneficial.

responsible for healthy, resilient functioning in subgroups with unexpectedly positive outcomes. Indeed, such subgroups may tell us a considerable amount about the very mechanisms responsible for both typical and atypical functioning. For example, in the investigation of HIV and AIDS, study of the small subset of individuals who show unusually strong resistance to infection with the virus has been essential in ascertaining that certain genes are responsible for such resilience, potentially leading to advances in genomics and the development of vaccines and treatments. The "pathological" and "healthy" poles of human existence need to be integrated, not dichotomized.

On the other hand, I can only speculate that it might have been beneficial for my father to have been able to share some of his worst experiences and darkest secrets during his early and middle years and to disclose the sense of shame he undoubtedly experienced. Indeed, such disclosure might have placed a dent in his lifelong self-image as "a psychotic." A growing field of research shows that the ability to express negative life events may have adaptive value for physical as well as mental functioning.[7] Key investigations in this paradigm reveal, for example, that maintaining diaries or otherwise writing about important, negative life experiences can have both immediate and lasting benefits for both psychological well-being and physical health, in contrast to similar writing about non-emotion-laden material. Along this line, I can't help but think that, as I matured and my father began to disclose his life's events to me, he experienced a kind of self-acceptance that he had perhaps not attained previously. Such acceptance was probably limited, however, by the lateness of the disclosure and the extreme care with which he chose to tell his son of many of his secrets.

Recent work in the study of resilience raises several provocative themes. For one thing, resilience goes beyond characteristics or traits inside the person; it is also the product of interactions with the environment. Family and relationship factors may promote resilient functioning, including, for children, the presence of at least one strong bond with an adult outside the family and, for an adult, partnership with a supportive mate or spouse. Indeed, without my mother's support, who knows where my father might have ended up? Yet this support was not supplemented by my father's ability or willingness to disclose his inner world and past experiences. Wider sources of support in the community are also relevant.[8] These would include, in the case of persons with serious mental disturbance, responsive after-care services following hospitalization. Such resources, however, were entirely lacking during and after all of my father's initial episodes; they are still woefully undersupported and underfunded in our society.

From a slightly different perspective, how caregivers and professionals react and respond to the individual with mental disorder (and, indeed, how society at large views mental illness) becomes a crucial factor regarding the promotion of resilience versus despair. How much more resilient might my father have been had institutions provided real care and had professionals respected him, explained clearly the nature of his disorder, and been able to supply him with effective treatments? Perhaps his cognitive decline would have been prevented or at least minimized. In this sense, fighting the stigma that pertains to mental disorder may well be the most critical means of helping those who suffer from its symptoms to attain healthy functioning.[9] The shame with which society views mental illness can only be internalized by the individual and his or her family members. In other words, fear and distancing on the part of social institutions and discriminatory practices on the part of governments and insurers are extremely likely to be mirrored by distancing and silence at the levels of patients and their closest supports.

Other sources of resilience are just beginning to be investigated. For example, provocative findings from recent years suggest that the propensity for mentally *healthy* functioning may have at least some genetic components.[10] Indeed, specific genetic loci may protect certain individuals born into strongly "loaded" families from displaying bipolar disorder.[11] Although resilience is usually thought of as psychological or social in nature, it is intriguing that at least some facets of resilience may be mediated by one's DNA.

As our field makes further efforts toward defining this elusive construct,[12] it is clear that what we do not know

190

about resilience still far outweighs what we do know. I close with two key points that emerge from this brief discussion. (1) Persons with mental disorder are essentially and irreducibly human; their similarities with everyone else vastly outweigh their differences. Considering and embracing such fundamental humanity may well be the most important attitude for professionals and, indeed, for all of society, not only for gaining a better understanding of resilience but also for reducing the stigma that still pervades opinions toward and responses to mental disorder. (2) Despite the very real suffering and loss induced by serious mental illness, a great many individuals so afflicted rise above their predispositions and legacies to lead productive, sensitive, and even inspiring lives. This phenomenon, along with other facets of healthy functioning, requires far more of the field's attention. A major scientific and clinical goal is to capture, much more sensitively and accurately than has been done to date, just what the components and processes underlying such resilience are likely to be. In short, and provocatively, the study of mental disorder may turn out to yield essential insights into optimal human functioning.

Inner and Outer Worlds

From most vantage points, mental disorder would appear to be primarily a private, individual phenomenon, afflicting the person's innermost thoughts and feelings and leading to behavior patterns that are often mysterious and inexplicable. But all of mental life, including the aberrant and disturbed, is deeply embedded in social and cultural context.

It is now widely accepted that severe mental disorders like schizophrenia and bipolar disorder are universal on our planet. They exist in all societies, with nearly identical prevalence rates across diverse cultures.[13] Both disorders have substantial heritabilities, with especially high figures in the case of bipolar disorder. Basic biological mechanisms are becoming far better known for each. Indeed, brain imaging is also yielding precise neural localization of hallucinatory and delusional experiences as well as neural regions and processes that may underlie severe mood disturbance.[14] Although far more needs to be learned, the underpinnings of these devastating disorders are yielding to scientific inquiry at ever-increasing rates.

Despite this growing sophistication in terms of psychobiological conceptualization, cultural and social factors have much to do with both the symptom content and the ultimate outcomes of these conditions. With regard to the latter, despite its undoubted biological basis, schizophrenia appears to have a markedly different prognosis across different societies. In fact, non-Western, nonindustrialized cultures, particularly those in Africa, reveal a more positive set of longterm outcomes for persons with schizophrenia than do industrialized societies like ours.[15] The possible reasons for this well-replicated finding appear to be that African societies have stronger mechanisms of social support and social connectedness than do most Western nations and that meaningful work roles are readily available there for those whose aberrant behavior has temporarily taken them out of the mainstream. The message is clear: Social context matters, even for disorders with undoubted biological origins.

In addition, the very forms that these disorders take, as well as the content of the pathological thinking characteristic of these conditions, are clearly shaped by social environment and context. The content of depressive rumination is typically related to loss experiences and to a person's unique history of interaction with the world.[16] In addition, psychotic experiences are related to cultural and historical forces. Indeed, my father's initial episode and suicide attempt were framed in terms of paranoid reactions to the rise of fascism, as was much of the imagery preceding his 1945 episode following his doctoral degree. Somehow he believed that if his life were sacrificed, Hitler's life would end as well.

I quoted earlier from the letter my father wrote in response to the inquiry he had received in the mid-1980s, soliciting his recollections of the Great Depression. At the end of his inquiry, the man who had asked for my father's opinions and recollections queried about the most striking memory from the Depression era. My father's reply was as follows:

> ... As to my most vivid memory of the times: The Depression was world-wide. My most vivid memories concern the rise of Nazi fascism. Many of us knew that World War II was highly likely if not inevitable. Yet with Quaker training from my father, I was a staunch Pacifist. These external world clashes led by Hitler and Mussolini became internalized in me. How could a birthright Quaker be a pacifist when democracy was threatened so harshly? But again, "Thou shalt not kill." Coupled with the achievement of puberty and with my continued search for self-identity and for God, the world situation seemed hopeless. I worried so much that for half of my 12th school year, I had to stay out of school to find myself again. A vivid memory indeed.

In reflecting on this passage, I first note the striking historical context of my father's initial episode. Reiterating a point I have made repeatedly, the content of psychotic experiences may well be tied to real conflicts, both personal and historical. I cannot also help but note, in passing, the dual meaning of the historical term "Great Depression."[17]

At a more psychological level, I read, between the lines, of my father's skillful – and not wholly fabricated – deflection of his absence from school to grave concerns about the world situation. I also infer, from the measured tones he used to mask the utter chaos he experienced, the great effort it took, throughout his life, to hide his episodes and hospitalizations and to cover over his most personal, profound experiences. With society's worst epithets and judgments reserved for those who behave in psychotic fashion, and with the utter lack of skilled, knowledgeable professional support for my father (and so many others like him), who can blame him for being extremely cautious with his choice of words and his omissions?

I also find it provocative that, during his 1945 hospitalization, he had the delusion that he was being housed in a concentration camp. He doubtless felt, at some level, as alone and cut off from hope as those who were warehoused, tortured, and executed overseas in those obscene settings. Did he wonder whether he would be strong enough, or lucky enough, to survive? Was he still identifying with victims of fascism? Despite their clear irrationality, psychotic symptoms can reflect real-world issues and concerns.

But the parallel cuts deeper. Indeed, Hitler's goals were to rid the world not only of Jewish people but also of people who were homosexual, Gypsies, and "mental defectives," including individuals suffering from major mental illness. In an important sense, then, my father's paranoid delusion was prescient, reflecting the reality that humans' capacities for hatred and discrimination are often directed strongly against persons with "different" thoughts and ideas, against those with vulnerabilities toward behaving irrationally, and against those with mental retardation or mental illness per se.

It appears that we, as a species, are "programmed" to probe for the in-group versus out-group status of fellow humans with whom we come in contact, because accurate recognition once meant (and can still mean, in warlike circumstances) survival.[18] In our initial probing of and scanning for salient features of our contacts, we tend to exaggerate and distort differences, even attributing subhuman qualities to those who are the most threatening. Indeed, as in the case of racism toward ethnic minorities, our fear of those with mental disorders has led to dehumanization throughout history, with resultant warehousing, enslavement, and even annihilation.[19]

Although our propensities for creating such in-groups and out-groups are deeply ingrained, they are still amenable to change. Patterns of racism have, in some instances, been reduced dramatically in the period of a generation, although clear divides still remain.[20] And there appears to be more compassion, at least in some quarters, toward the mentally ill than there was some decades, and certainly some centuries, ago. The key, in my view, is to prevent the potentially oppressed from being construed as subhuman. Indeed, when ethnic minorities or those afflicted with mental disorders are perceived as less than fully human, the potential for degradation, isolation, and even genocide is not far off.

What strategies might be invoked to counter the stigmatization of mental illness? Corrigan and Penn have described three main procedures: protests against discrimination, public education campaigns, and personal contact with afflicted persons.[21] As for the latter, the nature of the contact appears all-important. Visits to mental hospitals, in which "us versus them" roles can be magnified, are far less likely to engender positive attitude change than are meaningful interactions in community settings, in which egalitarian contacts are likely to be fostered. Yet such meaningful contacts can happen only when changes in policy, including far greater provision of community supports and aftercare, allow persons with mental disorder to have the opportunity for normalized community involvement.

To the list of Corrigan and Penn, I would add a fourth: disclosure. Indeed, as noted earlier, personal disclosure may have great benefits for the individual who speaks or writes about difficult life experiences.[22] Furthermore, public disclosure is increasingly part of the landscape as a key step on the road toward public acceptance and even fundraising and advocacy for medical disorders. Witness, for example, the many current "role models" for physical illnesses (e.g., Muhammad Ali and Michael J. Fox, who have publicly disclosed their struggles with Parkinson's disease). For mental disorder, a parallel may be found in the greatly increasing numbers of personal accounts that have appeared in written form.[23] Even visual media such as television and cinema have begun to bring mental disorder out of the "closet" in more realistic ways than ever before.[24] Although it is still far riskier to be viewed as crazy than physically ill, the barriers are slowly being crossed.

Societal reactions are mirrored in family reactions. If mental disorder is the subject of shame and degradation, families will react by blaming themselves as well as the afflicted individual. William Beardslee's admirable goal of having parents with depression develop narratives that can enhance their children's understanding of irritability, withdrawal, and other expressions of mood disorder provides a fine counterexample, with documented therapeutic and preventive benefits.[25] The alternative is for children to wonder and worry in silence, creating fertile ground for ignorance, fear, and self-blame.

At many levels, then, and reflecting the contextual nature of thought and behavior, mental disorder truly lies at the interface of inner and outer worlds. The hope is that greater understanding of mental illness at a scientific level, greater disclosure of mentally disordered experiences at personal and family levels, and greater acceptance of nonharmful social deviance (as well as greater provision of aftercare services) at cultural and societal levels can work synergistically, allowing increased knowledge, openness, and access to treatment and care as well as the formation of self-images that are positive and resilient as opposed to shameful and disgraced.

One thing is certain: Like the struggles for equality regarding ethnicity, sex, and sexual preference, the battle for reduced stigma and greater social acceptance of mental disorder will continue to be long and difficult. Progress is likely to be met by setbacks. Basic human tendencies to stereotype, distance, and segregate will need continuous efforts to be countered. I do not harbor the delusion that acceptance of unusual and inexplicable behavior will ever be complete. I still contend, however, that the fight is worthwhile, as progress on this front will signal an improved era for the personal well-being and social connectedness of all persons within a given society and across societies.

13

A Son's Perspective

In the spirit of disclosure, I raise several themes from my own life, which pertain chiefly to my upbringing and my relationship with my father. My goal here is to capture experiences that may be shared by other individuals who have been brought up in the context of severe mental disorder. The conflict between silence and control versus openness and disclosure is the major motif of these words. I also consider which aspects of the family legacy I may "carry," both genetically and psychologically, and I discuss issues regarding becoming a parent myself. I close with a brief discussion of the potential risks involved in making the disclosures in this work. Overall, although I have focused this book on my father, I believe that I would be neglectful if I failed to capture a bit more about my experiences as a son, including the reverberations of those experiences throughout my adult years.

Silence and Control

Several years ago, I shared an earlier version of the present work with a colleague, a gifted psychologist and psychotherapist. After she had read the draft, we planned a lunch meeting to discuss her reactions. Not only did she generously wish to give me some feedback, but my words had evidently brought up issues about her own family of origin.

I was anxious before our lunch meeting, given my uncertainty as to how she would react to my attempt to capture my father's story in writing. As I sat down at the table, the first thing she noted was that my work could have an alternate title. Puzzled, I asked what she had in mind. She replied that she would be tempted to rename the narrative "Just Don't Talk About It."

I wondered for a moment what she could possibly mean, before realizing that what had caught her attention was the utter silence in which I grew up. Still, it took me some time to grapple with her pronouncement. Were the off-limits nature of my father's absences, I wondered, and the lack of any discussion when he returned, actually that striking, that unusual? Was there really any other way? I simply couldn't fathom how a family might have done it any differently or how such topics could actually have been discussed. Only more recently have I fully realized that alternatives do indeed exist.

Deeply ingrained in me are several core stances: silence, not asking for help, figuring things out on my own, holding back, keeping control over my emotions and behavior. For much of my life, I have tended to cope by doing things rather than talking about them, by caretaking others rather than myself, and by reducing conflict rather than confronting issues that are unclear or that need resolution. Even today, I cringe when a group with whom I am interacting – workmates, colleagues, family members – shows open conflict, as I am fearful that the conflict will escalate and that I will not be able to handle it. I have tended to place a premium on harmony, or even the appearance of harmony, fearing that any expression of conflict will unearth deeper, uncontrollable reactions.

There is, of course, a huge price for such "management" of emotion: The underlying issues may never get discussed or dealt with. In addition, by preempting conflict in this way, issues may build to the point that any resolution comes too late if at all.

My habits seem to me to be a remnant of the utter control and silence, and the fear of underlying explosiveness, that permeated my childhood. Only gradually have I learned that confronting conflictual themes early in the chain of events can effect change and provide emotional grounding without engendering destruction. Writing this work is, in fact, part of the process of not being so silent, so accepting, so unquestioning.

But still, in contemplating my early years, I find it hard to imagine that things could really have been different. Might there actually have been ways other than just forging ahead and ignoring important questions, even those right in front of me? The entire social climate of the 1950s, I remind myself now, was one in which mental illness was not discussed. My father's psychiatrist instructed him not to talk with my sister and me about his affliction. In keeping with the tenor of the times, my mother declined to mention even to her own attorney the real reasons for her potential separation and divorce.

When I consider my early childhood, I recall almost no irrationality or out-of-control behavior in my father. He was either present, and largely himself; or absent altogether. When I was older, in junior high school and high school, I sometimes felt that his ideas were a bit "off" and I wondered about his living so much in his mind, as a philosopher. I was also puzzled by his occasional lack of activity, which I now believe to have been related to periods of flat depression, or his occasionally erratic behavior, symptomatic of hypomanic periods. Yet regarding his frequent and severe episodes in the 1950s and early 1960s, during my first decade of life, I have had to use historical knowledge gained from my parents during my adulthood to complete the picture and to fill in those empty spaces, which I barely knew at the time to be empty.

Thus, when asked to provide a reaction to growing up in the household of a parent with bipolar disorder, I think of my father's response to the historian's inquiry about life during the Great Depression, in which he stated that it was hard to respond because he did not know at the time that he was living in such an era. Thus, what was it like for me to live in the shadow of periodic, uncontrolled manic-depressive illness? I don't really know, I protest, because I wasn't conscious of the situation at the time. Or, at least, I wasn't aware of the irrationality, paranoia, and chaos underneath the surface.

But what *was* it like? For one thing, it was extremely quiet. I sensed that many topics just weren't discussed. It was so quiet, in fact, that I internalized the quietness and learned to ignore the questions I had, particularly those about my father's absences. Changing this underlying pattern has come slowly, well into my adult years.

Certainly, this pattern of silence was preferable to experiencing out-of-control, paranoid, or irrational behavior head-on. Indeed, for most of my adult life, since the time that I became more fully aware of my father's condition through our conversations and through talks with my mother, I have held to the belief that I came out relatively unscathed from the aftermath of my childhood. Whatever genetic "loading" for bipolar disorder I may carry, I have somehow escaped its impact. Furthermore, I tell myself, my parents hid the worst of his episodes from me and from my sister; my father kept his professorship; and my family coped as best they could, particularly in light of the doctors' clear messages to not inform the children. Thus, there was no real trauma to suppress, no fights or violence that might have damaged me. My childhood was, in fact, far more benign than the childhoods of countless children from far worse backgrounds, including those born into poverty, those whose parents are absent altogether, or those who have had to witness irrational, out-of-control behavior first-hand. And, most tellingly, I have never had to experience personally the terror of psychosis, the utter loss of control of mania, or the unrelenting despair of chronic depression.

Indeed, throughout my life I have nearly always been the "stable" one, the responsible one, in most family and work situations. If anything, I tend to take on too much responsibility, probably a vestige of my need to maintain control and to succeed. Overall, I marvel at my good fortune, wondering from time to time how I escaped the worst elements of the family legacy.

But has the picture really been this benign? Is it possible to be completely sheltered, as a child, from the effects of such devastating psychoses as my father had, even if most of the direct "messages" were covered over? Did I detect, at some level, elements of rage or madness that I did not consciously experience? And how much has the legacy of silence and control that I experienced throughout childhood persisted?

Certainly, I was protected from the blunt impact of my father's episodes, through what I now understand to have been nearly superhuman control on the part of my parents. Yet what might have seeped through this facade, this heroic but ultimately misguided attempt toward control?

One thing from which I could not be protected was the loneliness that accompanied the silence. I was a fairly self-sufficient boy, at an emotional level, but I often felt that there was no one I could really speak with about what I felt. I kept the feelings inside; I maintained control, as best I could. The cost in terms of loneliness and silent suffering was sometimes palpable, as the story of my initial year in organized baseball, frozen in right field, reveals (see opening words to Chapter 6).

Much later, during college, I experienced serious and real conflict over sleep and control, developing a pattern of induced vomiting that began to threaten my health. I let the pattern continue for far too long, with the silence in which I grew up a familiar companion during my stressful days and nights, during which I struggled horribly and self-punitively. Part of the problem was that I was too ashamed and too proud to ask for real help.

In recent years, I have talked with a close friend, a talented psychotherapist and neuropsychologist, about my early experiences. He has emphasized emphatically that family members can't ever escape the full impact of psychotic experiences as severe as those my father experienced. Even if the symptoms were hidden, the efforts to hide them must inevitably have taken a toll. The bravery that my mother showed; the unreal control that my father displayed when he was in front of my sister and me; the utter lack of communication about out-of-control feelings and experiences that my parents both endured: Somehow I picked up on the "fact," in my family, that some things are too dangerous to touch, to feel, to explore, or certainly to discuss.

Overall, regarding disclosure to children who live with mental disorder in their families, there must be a "middle ground" between exposure to chaos, on the one hand, and deafening silence, on the other, a middle ground that would involve the parents' ability to create a meaningful story, in words that the child or adolescent could comprehend, to help explain the home situation. As I have commented earlier, this component of Beardslee's family treatment has been associated with documented treatment gains for the family and even with prevention of future mood disorder in the offspring. Of course, some families in which parents suffer from chronic psychoses or other severe psychopathology may not be able to create such a narrative; the child will require other supports outside the home. Furthermore, no family that is potentially able to work with their children in such a way will be motivated to seek treatment if the fact of having a mental disorder continues to be viewed as shameful and something to hide. In other words, there must be a mutual interplay of changed attitudes within families *and* within society regarding attitudes toward mental disorder.

The Family Legacy

What of other aspects of my legacy? I have come to see that although my moods are usually quite stable, I am susceptible to two-to-three-day long periods of sadness and isolation, when the world appears to me to be caving in. These periods appear with some regularity, though a bit less so in recent years. I keep these moods from all but my closest contacts, but they are real. I see these time periods as a pale remnant of the volatile temperament that is part of my genetic inheritance.

At another level, I also believe that such moods reflect a deep fear of being abandoned, whether through simply noticing (without explanation) my father's absences as a child or picking up on the omissions in my mother's words and experiences. Today, saying goodbye to anyone, even for a short period of time, can bring up in me a momentary sense of panic that is clearly irrational and that I now know to expect. But it is still there.

Tellingly, in my adult life, following breakups of key relationships, I have twice crossed over from expected bereavement and sadness into major depression. In each case, the energy I usually possess utterly left me, and I became nearly immobilized by anxiety and hopelessness. Are such bouts the result of a genetic predisposition? Or is fear of abandonment the key issue? My guess is that both seeds are present. Fortunately, I have had access to psychotherapy, and on each occasion antidepressant medications provided needed stability for a month or two.

I must point out that the experience of depression, even if for relatively short time periods, has produced empathy in me for those who fall victim to mood disorders and other forms of mental disturbance, an empathy that far surpasses all of the clinical training and book learning I have ever received. I do not believe that formation of empathy results solely from having extreme life experiences, but I do think that being in touch with sadness is a prerequisite for understanding another's level of pain.

What about any manic or hypomanic tendencies in me? Even raising the issue brings up an internal protest: I have been so controlled in my life and work – hyperresponsible, as caretaker, teacher/professor, and camp director – that the depiction seems almost entirely out of place. But I do have a great deal of energy. I work on several projects at once, read several books at a time, accomplish many tasks each day related to teaching, research, and family life, and I thrive on the interplay of people, ideas, and constant mental juggling and prioritizing to keep it all afloat. I also like to immerse myself in complex ideas and thoughts, with utter excitement over the richness of the world and the opportunity to widen my all-too-limited understanding of it. I sometimes "surge" for several days, needing less sleep than usual as I near completion of an important project. Perhaps some of these tendencies are subclinical manifestations of my father's proclivities, but it would be a distortion to say that I have experienced mania or hypomania, or even cyclothymia (a less severe, cyclic variant of bipolar disorder). Yet I have doubtless benefited from some of the intensity and energy that are part of the family pattern.

Another aspect of the legacy is the worry about being a parent: How much risk does my son Jeffrey have for developing a severe mood disorder? Have I transmitted genetic vulnerability? Has his environment been sufficiently stable? The best answer is that no one knows, at least in the field's present state of knowledge. Encouragingly, even with the strong heritability of bipolar disorder, the risk to the child of an afflicted parent is still low, on the order of 10 percent.[1] Only time will tell with regard to Jeffrey, but it is not an issue that I dwell on. I have a strong sense that he will continue to develop well, as he has done so far; and that if intervention were ever needed as he proceeds through adolescence and adulthood, he would receive it quickly. As a parent, I have come to the conclusion that the only stance to take is one of confidence and support. This growing confidence carried me through a difficult time of separation and divorce, following my father's death, and strengthened my conviction that my new, second marriage will only bolster my motivation and skills as a parent.

The Current Disclosure

What might be the impact of having the words I have written herein appear in print? There is a large part of me that would like to believe that there will be no negative ramifications whatsoever, that the mental health field and the general public have become sufficiently open to disclosures of mental disorder in oneself or one's family that this work will simply become part of a growing testimony of personal and family accounts. On the other hand, this view may be naive, particularly with respect to reactions of others in the helping professions.

Kay Jamison, for example, received a significant amount of distressingly negative reaction following the publication of her landmark autobiography, *An Unquiet Mind*, with some colleagues and professionals among the most critical of her disclosure.[2] There is, in fact, a clear tendency for professionals to convey discriminatory, hostile, nonaccepting attitudes toward those afflicted with mental disorders. Indeed, family members report that some of the greatest stigmatization they have experienced often emanates from those charged with helping the relative receiving treatment.[3] It may be that those responsible for treating persons with mental disorders distance themselves too greatly from the afflictions of those in their care, exemplified by extremes of "us versus them" thinking and attitudes. A fellow professional's disclosure, from this perspective, is tantamount to admitting a huge personal or familial flaw.

In fact, what should the standards be for the mental health of those working in the field? Does the presence of any mental disorder disqualify an individual from serving in such a role? My answer would be, in this regard, "of course not," given the high prevalence of such disorders as depression and anxiety disorders in the general population and the distinct possibility that personal experience with such conditions could actually enhance empathy and support. Yet what if the mental disorder in question involves severe levels of depression or psychotic levels of functioning, which could compromise the professional's ability to work and exhibit sound judgment? Should patients be exposed to the potential irrationality of providers with thought disorder, which can, as I took pains to explain earlier in this work, often accompany severe manias and depressions? And what of serious, judgment-impairing levels of substance abuse on the part of professionals?

Jamison, in fact, has set up a system of monitoring and consultation related to the possibility of "breakthrough" episodes that she may encounter despite her continued taking of mood-stabilizing medication. Clearly, she has given the entire issue considerable thought, challenging the field to do the same.[4]

More generally, there may be those who believe that it is not appropriate or even ethical for someone in clinical psychology (or a related helping profession) to divulge a family and personal history as "loaded" as mine. My response is that, on the contrary, modeling of openness and appropriate disclosure may constitute a large step on the road toward breaking the silence that still surrounds the topic of mental disorder and toward the destigmatization of psychological and psychiatric pathology. It would be a small group of professionals and scientists, indeed, who could claim that no mental illness is present in themselves or their immediate and extended families. Whereas basic standards of psychological competence may need to be enforced for practicing clinicians, in order that the public not be exposed to unsound judgment related to clear irrationality, there is grave danger in insisting on "clean bills of mental health" for those entering and practicing in the field.

Overall, I hope for a time, in the not too distant future, when disclosure of mental afflictions in oneself or one's family members would not be considered particularly brave. Such disclosures could certainly be thought of as important, sensitive, and poignant; but the designation as brave or heroic only reinforces the strong stigma that still surrounds the topic. Indeed, such a time period would signify a dramatic reduction in the stigmatization surrounding disorders that society still perceives as morally culpable, flawed, and reprehensible.

Coda

I have visited my father's gravesite, at the rural edge of Columbus, during several different seasons since his death. That first winter, in December of 1995, accompanied by my mother on a frigid but incredibly clear day following a snowstorm, I had to chip and cut away at ice and snow for many minutes before I could find his marker. With my son Jeffrey, on other visits during summer and early autumn seasons, I have recalled the hot July day of my father's burial. Although sad, I am peaceful during those visits, because I remember the connections that we had formed during our conversations, tracing my coming of age to his gradual revelations to me.

I occasionally wonder, during and after those gravesite visits, how his body is faring inside its casket, ravaged as it was during his last months of devastation from the end stages of Parkinson's and dementia. But I don't dwell on morbid thoughts. Rather, I feel almost peaceful, with the realization of what he gave me.

Sometimes my memory of my father seems cloudy, as I struggle to bring back those moments of our closest contact. Yet at other times, he is as real to me as if I had seen him yesterday. Perhaps his true legacy lies less in specific memories and more in my work in psychology, my teaching of students at Berkeley, and my research efforts with children suffering from mental and emotional

209

disorders. Or maybe the legacy is most present in my struggles for greater authenticity with others, including my family.

What I think of most, however, is our talks, those discussions that began during my first spring break in college, after I'd given him The Divided Self *for Christmas, awkwardly letting him know that I sensed something about those deeply troubled episodes of his life. I think of those occasions, in his study or in the car, when time outside the room would disappear, and the only thing that mattered was his words and the images they created: scenes of madness, of experiences beyond my imagining; active wondering about religion and philosophy; my father's probing for under-standing of his fate. Difficult as they sometimes were and as anxious as I sometimes was, I miss that level of contact. I miss those talks.*

Perhaps the ultimate bipolarity in me entails my strong tendencies toward silence and denial versus my gradual discovery of a voice with which to clarify my father's life as well as my own. Even as I write these closing words, the tension is still here: Do I open up my father's history, and some of my own deepest experiences, to others? Or do I keep it all inside? Will disclosure be indulgent, even destructive, or can it potentially serve to enlighten? My main wish is that I have communicated clearly about what I learned from the most intimate and dis-closing gift I have ever received: my father's opening up to me about his life and his experiences with mental disorder.

As any scientist knows, the study of a single case has a host of limitations. Yet intimate knowledge of a person's life may well be the best starting point from which to base a human, hu-mane, and ultimately rigorous science of etiology, treatment, prevention, and policy. I hope that I have been able to fulfill my main goal – to bear witness – in a sensitive and meaningful way.

Coda

The ultimate legacy of misdiagnosis, maltreatment, and denial of the realities of mental disorder is to take those profoundly affecting and disorganizing experiences of mental illness and to bury them where no further light can be shed, perpetuating, at both individual and societal levels, fear and distancing. My fervent hope is that this narrative and commentary have helped instead to encourage acceptance and approach, and to uncover, rather than bury, both the painful and the uplifting elements of my father's life. Recounting my father's story is a small step toward "coming out," toward promoting openness, with the objective of breaking the cycle of silence and denial that still surround, envelop, and banish mental disorder.

I am thankful for my father's presence in my life and for the opportunity to share his story. I wish strength and courage to any readers who have experienced, in themselves or in their families, the particularly searing and disabling pain of mental disorder. I hope for a more enlightened future for all persons and family members so touched and so afflicted, although I am well aware that it will take considerable disclosure, courage, wisdom, and patience for such a future to become a reality. Although they cannot convey all that my father felt or dealt with, all that my family had to bear, or all that I have come to learn, the words herein are a small attempt to give meaning to the often-chaotic experiences of my father's life and to ensure that the harrowing as well as uplifting messages emanating from that life are not silenced.

Notes

Introduction

1. E. R. Kandel and L. R. Squire, "Neuroscience: Breaking Down Scientific Barriers to the Study of Brain and Mind," *Science* 290 (2000): 1113–20.
2. For writings on stigma and mental disorder, see S. P. Hinshaw and D. Cicchetti, "Stigma and mental Disorder: Conceptions of Illness, Public Attitudes, Personal Disclosure, and Social Policy," *Development and Psychopathology* 12 (2000): 555–98; and O. F. Wahl, *Telling Is Risky Business: Mental Health Consumers Confront Stigma* (New Brunswick, N.J.: Rutgers University Press, 1999).
3. U.S. Department of Health and Human Services, *Mental Health: A Report of the Surgeon General* (Rockville, Md.: published by the author, 1999).
4. C. J. Murray and A. D. Lopez, eds., *The Global Burden of Disease: A Comprehensive Assessment of Mortality and Disability from Diseases, Injuries, and Risk Factors in 1990 and Projected to 2020* (Cambridge, Mass.: Harvard School of Public Health, 1996).
5. http://www.NoStigma.com.
6. http://www.rcpsych.ac.uk.
7. R. Pear, "Drive for Mental Health Coverage Fails in Congress," *New York Times*, December 18, 2001, p. A18.
8. R. Sommer, J. S. Clifford, and J. C. Norcross, "A Bibliography of Mental Patients' Autobiographies: An Update and Classification System," *American Journal of Psychiatry* 155 (1998): 1261–64. Recently, searing personal accounts of depression have been combined with incisive commentary on the nature of depressive disorder in A. Solomon, *The Noonday Demon: An Atlas of Depression* (New York: Scribner, 2001);

and J. Smith, *Where the Roots Reach for Water: A Personal and Natural History of Melancholia* (New York: North Point Press, 1999).
9. N. Lachenmeyer, *The Outsider* (New York: Random House, 2000); J. Neugeboren, *Imagining Robert: My Brother, Madness, and Survival* (New York: Henry Holt, 1988).
10. O. F. Wahl, *Telling Is Risky Business: Mental Health Consumers Confront Stigma* (New Brunswick, N.J.: Rutgers University Press, 1999).

1. Beginnings

1. K. R. Jamison, *Touched with Fire: Manic-Depressive Illness and the Artistic Temperament* (New York: Free Press, 1993).
2. E. R. Kandel and L. R. Squire, "Neuroscience: Breaking Down the Scientific Barriers to the Study of Brain and Mind," 290 (2000): 1113–20; R. Plomin and J. Crabbe, "DNA," *Psychological Bulletin* 126 (2000): 806–28.

4. Professorship and Family

1. J. Gleick, *Genius: The Life and Physics of Richard Feynman* (New York: Vintage, 1992).
2. V. G. Hinshaw, Jr., "The Epistemological Relevance of Mannheim's Sociology of Knowledge," *Journal of Philosophy* 40 (1944): 57–72; V. G. Hinshaw, Jr., "The Pragmatist Theory of Truth," *Philosophy of Science* 11 (1944): 82–92.
3. V. G. Hinshaw, Jr., "Einstein's Social Philosophy," in P. A. Schilpp, ed., *Albert Einstein: Philosopher-Scientist* (Evanston, Ill.: Library of Living Philosophers, 1949), 647–61.

5. The '50s: An Uphill Battle

1. F. K. Goodwin and K. R. Jamison, *Manic-Depressive Illness* (New York: Oxford University Press, 1990).
2. T. Burt, J. Prudic, S. Peyser, and S. Clark, et al., "Learning and Memory in Bipolar and Unipolar Major Depression: Effects of Aging," *Neuropsychiatry, Neuropsychology, and Behavioral Neurology* 13 (2000): 246–53; H. A. Sackeim, "Memory and ECT: From Polarization to Reconciliation," *Journal of ECT* 16 (2000): 87–96.
3. R. C. Clodfelter and D. M. McDowell, "Bipolar Disorder and Substance Abuse: Consideration of Etiology, Comorbidity, Evaluation, and Treatment," *Psychiatric Annals* 31 (2001): 294–99.

4. U.S. Department of Health and Human Services, *Mental Health: A Report of the Surgeon General* (Rockville, Md.: published by the author, 1999).

7. Diagnosis and Misdiagnosis

1. The authoritative text of F. K. Goodwin and K. R. Jamison, *Manic-Depressive Illness* (New York: Oxford University Press, 1990), is the best guide in the field; the second edition is forthcoming. See also: F. M. Mondimore, *Bipolar Disorder: A Guide for Patients and Families* (Baltimore, Md.: Johns Hopkins University Press, 1999); L. P. Rehm, A. L. Wagner, and C. Ivens-Tyndol, "Mood Disorders: Unipolar and Bipolar," in P. B. Sutker and H. E. Adams, eds., *Comprehensive Handbook of Psychopathology*, 3rd ed. (New York: Kluwer Academic/Plenum, 2001), 277–308; and P. C. Whybrow, *A Mood Apart: Depression, Mania, and Other Afflictions of the Self* (New York: Basic Books, 1997).
2. American Psychiatric Association, *Diagnostic and Statistical Manual of Mental Disorders*, 4th ed. (Washington, D.C.: American Psychiatric Press, 1994).
3. G. A. Carlson and F. K. Goodwin, "The Stages of Mania: A Longitudinal Analysis of the Manic Episode," *Archives of General Psychiatry* 28 (1973): 221–28.
4. In those cases of bipolar disorder where episodes begin during childhood or early adolescence, clear-cut episodes of mania versus depression do not usually occur. Rather, the cycles are often "ultra-rapid" (on the order of every few days) or even "ultradian," with sudden switches from grandiosity to despair occurring several times per day (see B. Geller and J. Luby, "Child and Adolescent Bipolar Disorder: A Review of the Past 10 Years," *Journal of the American Academy of Child and Adolescent Psychiatry* 36 (1997): 1169–76).
5. R. J. Wyatt and I. Henter, "An Economic Evaluation of Manic-Depressive Illness," *Social Psychiatry and Psychiatric Epidemiology* 30 (1995): 213–19.
6. Goodwin and Jamison, *Manic Depressive Illness*.
7. Essential reading on suicide and its linkages with severe psychiatric disturbances such as bipolar disorder is found in K. R. Jamison, *Night Falls Fast: Understanding Suicide* (New York: Knopf, 1999).
8. Goodwin and Jamison, *Manic Depressive Illness*.
9. Whybrow, *A Mood Apart*.
10. For more information on seasonality, see Goodwin and Jamison, *Manic Depressive Illness*.
11. S. H. Barondes, *Mood Genes: Hunting for the Origins of Mania and Depression* (New York: W. H. Freeman, 1998).

12. S. L. Johnson and I. Miller, "Negative Life Events and Time to Recovery from Episodes of Bipolar Disorder," *Journal of Abnormal Psychology* 106 (1997): 449–57; S. L. Johnson and J. E. Roberts, "Life Events and Bipolar Disorder: Implications from Biological Theories," *Psychological Bulletin* 117 (1995): 434–49; S. Malkoff-Schwartz, E. Frank, B. Anderson, J. T. Sherrill, L. Siegel, D. Patterson, and D. J. Kupfer, "Stressful Life Events and Social Rhythm Disruption in the Onset of Manic and Depressive Bipolar Episodes," *Archives of General Psychiatry* 55 (1998): 702–7.

13. R. M. Post, "Transduction of Psychosocial Stress into the Neurobiology of Recurrent Affective Disorder," *American Journal of Psychiatry* 149 (1992): 999–1010; R. M. Post, G. S. Leverich, G. Xing, and S. R. B. Weiss, "Developmental Vulnerabilities to the Onset and Course of Bipolar Disorder," *Development and Psychopathology* 13 (2001): 581–98.

14. J. M. Neale and T. Oltmanns, *Schizophrenia* (New York: Wiley, 1980).

15. E. Kraepelin, *Manic-Depressive Insanity and Paranoia* (1921; English ed., Edinburgh: Livingston, 1987).

16. Neale and Oltmanns, *Schizophrenia*.

17. J. K. Wing, J. E. Cooper, and N. Sartorius, *The Measurement and Classification of Psychiatric Symptoms* (Cambridge, Eng.: Cambridge University Press, 1974).

18. American Psychiatric Association, *Diagnostic and Statistical Manual of Mental Disorders*, 3rd ed. (Washington, D.C.: American Psychiatric Press, 1980).

19. American Psychiatric Association, *Diagnostic and Statistical Manual of Mental Disorders*, 4th ed.

20. M. Schou, "Prophylactic Lithium Treatment of Unipolar and Bipolar Manic-Depressive Illness," *Psychopathology* 28 (1995): 81–85.

21. M. Schou, "Forty Years of Lithium Treatment," *Archives of General Psychiatry* 54 (1997): 9–13.

22. P. C. Baastrup and M. Schou, "Lithium as a Prophylactic Agent: Its Effect against Recurrent Depression and Manic-Depressive Psychosis," *Archives of General Psychiatry* 16 (1969): 162–72.

23. N. C. Andreasen, "Changing Concepts of Schizophrenia and the Ahistorical Fallacy," *American Journal of Psychiatry* 151 (1994): 1405–7.

24. For a striking example related to Nobel laureate John Nash, see S. Nasar, *A Beautiful Mind* (New York: Simon and Schuster, 1998).

25. M. A. Taylor, "Are Schizophrenia and Affective Disorder Related? A Selective Literature Review," *American Journal of Psychiatry* 149 (1992): 22–32.

26. K. D. Denicoff, S. O. Ali, A. F. Mirsky, E. E. Smith-Jackson, G. S. Leverich, C. C. Duncan, E. G. Connell, and R. M. Post, "Relationship between Prior Course of Illness and Neuropsychological Functioning in

Patients with Bipolar Disorder," *Journal of Affective Disorders* 56 (1999): 67–73; W. G. van Gorp, L. Altshuler, D. C. Theberge, J. Wilkins, and W. Dixon, "Cognitive Impairment in Euthymic Bipolar Patients with and without Prior Alcohol Dependence," *Archives of General Psychiatry* 55 (1998): 41–46.

27. Barondes, *Mood Genes.*
28. P. E. Meehl, "Why I Do Not Attend Case Conferences," in P. E. Meehl, ed., *Psychodiagnosis: Selected Papers* (New York: W.W. Norton, 1973), 225–302.
29. S. A. Kirk and H. Hutchins, "Is Bad Writing a Mental Disorder?" *New York Times*, June 20, 1994.
30. See, e.g., P. R. Breggin, *Brain-Disabling Treatments in Psychiatry: Drugs, Electroshock, and the Role of the FDA* (New York: Springer, 1997).
31. Whybrow, *A Mood Apart.*

8. Disclosure and New Diagnosis

1. R. D. Laing, *The Divided Self: A Study in Sanity and Madness* (Baltimore, Md.: Penguin, 1965).

9. Waning Powers

1. R. L. Richards, D. C. Kinney, I. Lunde, M. Benet, and A. P. Merzel, "Creativity in Manic-Depressives, Cyclothymes, Their Normal Relatives, and Control Subjects," *Journal of Abnormal Psychology* 97 (1988): 281–88.
2. P. C. Baastrup and M. Schou, "Lithium as a Prophylactic Agent: Its effect against Recurrent Depression and Manic Depressive Psychosis," *Archives of General Psychiatry* 16 (1969): 162–72.
3. W. E. Craighead, D. J. Miklowitz, F. C. Vajk, and E. Frank, "Psychosocial Treatments for Bipolar Disorder," in P. E. Nathan and J. M. Gorman, eds., *A Guide to Treatments That Work* (New York: Oxford University Press, 1998), 240–48.
4. The dissertation studies were published as (1) S. P. Hinshaw, B. Henker, and C. K. Whalen, "Self-Control in Hyperactive Boys in Anger-Inducing Situations: Effects of Cognitive-Behavioral Training and of Methylphenidate," *Journal of Abnormal Child Psychology* 12 (1984): 55–77; and (2) S. P. Hinshaw, B. Henker, and C. K. Whalen, "Cognitive-Behavioral and Pharmacologic Interventions for Hyperactive Boys: Comparative and Combined Effects," *Journal of Consulting and Clinical Psychology* 52 (1984): 739–49.

5. American Psychiatric Association (1980).
6. E. Goffman, *Asylums: Essays on the Social Situations of Mental Patients and Other Inmates* (New York: Doubleday, 1961); R. D. Laing, *The Politics of Experience* (New York: Pantheon, 1967).
7. See discussion in S. P. Hinshaw and D. Cicchetti, "Stigma and Mental Disorder: Conceptions of Illness, Public Attitudes, Personal Disclosure, and Social Policy," *Development and Psychopathology* 12 (2000): 555–98.
8. U.S. Department of Health and Human Services, *Mental Health: A Report of the Surgeon General* (Rockville, Md.: published by the author, 1999).

10. Final Years

1. T. M. Dawson, "Parkinson's Disease: Clinical Manifestations and Treatment," *International Review of Psychiatry* 12 (2000): 263–69.

11. Causes and Treatments

1. S. H. Barondes, *Mood Genes: Hunting for the Origins of Mania and Depression* (New York: Freeman, 1998); F. K. Goodwin and K. R. Jamison, *Manic Depressive Illness* (New York: Oxford University Press, 1990).
2. M. Rutter, "Genetic Studies of Autism: From the 1970s into the Millennium," *Journal of Abnormal Child Psychology* 28 (2000): 3–14; R. Tannock, "Attention Deficit Hyperactivity Disorder: Advances in Cognitive, Neurobiological, and Genetic Research," *Journal of Child Psychology and Psychiatry* 39 (1998): 65–99.
3. J. A. Egeland, D. S. Gerhard, D. L. Pauls, J. N. Sussex, et al., "Bipolar Affective Disorder's Linkage to DNA Markers on Chromosome 11," *Nature* 325 (1987): 783–87; J. R. Kelsoe, E. F. Ginns, J. A. Egeland, D. S. Gerhard, et al., "Re-evaluation of the Linkage between Chromosome 11p Loci and the Gene for Bipolar Affective Disorder in the Old Order Amish," *Nature* 342 (1989): 238–43.
4. E. Goode, "Most Ills Are a Matter of More Than One Gene," *New York Times*, June 27, 2000, pp. D1, D6; R. A. Philibert, J. A. Egeland, S. M. Paul, and E. I. Ginnes, "The Inheritance of Bipolar Affective Disorder: Abundant Genes Coming Together," *Journal of Affective Disorders* 43 (1997): 1–3.
5. Barondes, *Mood Genes.*
6. P. McGuffin, B. Riley, and R. Plomin, "Toward Behavioral Genomics," *Science* 291 (2001): 1232, 1249; M. Ridley, *Genome: The Autobiography of a Species in 23 Chapters* (New York: HarperCollins, 1999).

7. G. Gottlieb, "Normally Occurring Environmental and Behavioral Influences on Genetic Activity: From Central Dogma to Probabilistic Epigenesis," *Psychological Review* 105 (1998): 792–802.
8. M. Rutter and the English and Romanian Adoptees (ERA) Study Team, "Developmental Catch-Up, and Deficit, Following Adoption after Severe Early Privation," *Journal of Child Psychology and Psychiatry* 39 (1998): 465–76.
9. R. M. Post, "Transduction of Psychosocial Stress into the Neurobiology of Recurrent Affective Disorder," *American Journal of Psychiatry* 149 (1992): 999–1010.
10. For research evidence, see L. Johnson, G. Andersson-Lundman, A. Aberg-Wistedt, and A. A. Mathe, "Age of Onset in Affective Disorder: Its Correlation with Hereditary and Psychosocial Factors," *Journal of Affective Disorders* 52 (1999): 139–48.
11. Barondes, *Mood Genes;* P. C. Whybrow, *A Mood Apart: Depression, Mania, and Other Afflictions of the Self* (New York: Basic Books, 1997).
12. See, e.g., G. E. Barnes and H. Prosin, "Parental Death and Depression", *Journal of Abnormal Psychology* 94 (1985): 64–69; T. A. Furukawa, A. Ogura, T. Hirai, and S. Furihara, "Early Parental Deprivation Experiences among Patients with Bipolar Disorder and Major Depression: A Case-Control Study," *Journal of Affective Disorders* 52 (1999): 85–91; and E. Maier and M. E. Lachman, "Consequences of Early Parental Loss and Separation for Health and Well-Being in Midlife," *International Journal of Behavioral Development* 24 (2000): 183–89.
13. K. A. Kendall-Tackett, L. M. Williams, and D. Finkelhor, "Impact of Sexual Abuse on Children: A Review and Synthesis of Empirical Findings," *Psychological Bulletin* 113 (1993): 164–80; C. Wekerle and D. A. Wolfe, "Child Maltreatment," in E. J. Mash and R. A. Barkley, eds., *Child Psychopathology* (New York: Guilford Press, 1996), 492–537. In addition, there is compelling evidence that physical abuse in childhood is predictive of aggressive behavior patterns in the offspring, as reviewed in J. D. Coie and K. A. Dodge, "Aggression and Antisocial Behavior," in N. Eisenberg, ed., *Handbook of Child Psychology,* vol. 3: *Social, Emotional, and Personality Development* (New York: Wiley, 1998), 779–862.
14. R. M. Post, G. S. Leverich, G. Xing, and S. R. B. Weiss, "Developmental Vulnerabilities to the Onset and Course of Bipolar Disorder," *Development and Psychopathology* 13 (2001): 581–98.
15. For a review, see S. L. Johnson and J. E. Roberts, "Life Events and Bipolar Disorder: Implications from Biological Theories," *Psychological Bulletin* 117 (1995): 434–49.

16. S. Malkoff-Schwartz, E. Frank, B. Anderson, J. T. Sherill, L. Siegel, D. Patterson and D. J. Kupfer, "Stressful Life Events and Social Rhythm Disruption in the Onset of Manic and Depressive Episodes," *Archives of General Psychiatry* 55 (1998): 702–7.

17. S. L. Johnson and I. Miller, "Negative Life Events and Time to Recovery from Bipolar Disorder," *Journal of Abnormal Psychology* 106 (1997): 449–57.

18. D. Cicchetti and T. D. Cannon, "Neurodevelopmental Processes in the Ontogenesis and Epigenesis of Psychopathology," *Development and Psychopathology* 11 (1999): 375–93; D. J. Miklowitz and L. Alloy, "Psychosocial Factors in the Course and Treatment of Bipolar Disorder: Introduction to the Special Section," *Journal of Abnormal Psychology* 108 (1999): 555–57.

19. Whybrow, *A Mood Apart.*

20. Y. B. Davenport and M. L. Adland, "Postpartum Psychoses in Female and Male Bipolar Manic-Depressive Patients," *American Journal of Orthopsychiatry* 52 (1982): 288–97.

21. W. G. van Gorp, L. Altshuler, D. C. Theberge, J. Wilkins, and W. Dixon, "Cognitive Impairment in Euthymic Bipolar Patients with and without Prior Alcohol Dependence," *Archives of General Psychiatry* 55 (1998): 41–46.

22. W. Coryell, W. Scheftner, B. Keller, J. Endicott, J. Maser, and G. L. Klerman, "The Enduring Psychosocial Consequences of Mania and Depression," *American Journal of Psychiatry* 150 (1993): 720–27.

23. R. M. Post, "Transduction of Psychosocial Stress into the Neurobiology of Recurrent Affective Disorders," *American Journal of Psychiatry* 149 (1992): 999–1010.

24. American Psychiatric Association, *Practice Guideline for the Treatment of Patients with Bipolar Disorder*, Supplement (December 1994) to the *American Journal of Psychiatry*.

25. P. E. Keck and S. L. McElroy, "Pharmacological Treatment of Bipolar Disorders," in P. E. Nathan and J. M. Gorman, eds., *A Guide to Treatments That Work* (New York: Oxford University Press, 1998), 249–69; R. J. Baldessarini and L. Tondo, "Does Lithium Treatment Still Work? Evaluation of Stable Responses over Three Decades," *Archives of General Psychiatry* 57 (2000): 187–90.

26. M. Schou, "The Effectiveness of Prophylactic Lithium on Mortality and Suicidal Behavior: A Review for Clinicians," *Journal of Affective Disorders* 50 (1998): 253–59.

27. Goodwin and Jamison, *Manic Depressive Illness*; J. Mendlewicz, D. Souery, and S. K. Rivelli, "Short-Term and Long-Term Treatment for

Bipolar Patients: Beyond the Guidelines," *Journal of Affective Disorders* 55 (1999): 79–85.

28. W. E. Craighead, D. J. Miklowitz, F. C. Vajk, and E. Frank, "Psychosocial Treatments for Bipolar Disorder," in Nathan and Gorman, eds., *A Guide to Treatments That Work*, 240–48.

29. F. M. Mondimore, *Bipolar Disorder: A Guide for Patients and Families* (Baltimore, Md.: Johns Hopkins University Press, 1999).

30. J. F. Clarkin, D. Carpenter, J. Hull, P. Wilner, and I. Glick, "Effects of Psychoeducational Intervention for Married Patients with Bipolar Disorder and Their Spouses," *Psychiatric Services* 49 (1998): 531–33.

31. T. L. Simoneau, D. J. Miklowitz, J. A. Richards, R. Saleem, and E. L. George, "Bipolar Disorder and Family Communication: Effects of a Psychoeducational Treatment Program," *Journal of Abnormal Psychology* 108 (1999): 588–97.

32. E. Goffman, *Asylums: Essays on the Social Situations of Mental Patients and Other Inmates* (New York: Doubleday, 1961).

33. U.S. Department of Health and Human Services, *Mental Health: A Report of the Surgeon General* (Rockville, Md.: published by the author, 1999). Such lack of access is particularly relevant for members of ethnic minority groups, as documented in the supplement to the Surgeon General's Report: U.S. Department of Health and Human Services, *Mental Health: Culture, Race, and Ethnicity – A Supplement to Mental Health: A Report of the Surgeon General* (Rockville, Md.: published by the author, 2001).

34. O. F. Wahl, *Telling Is Risky Business: Mental Health Consumers Confront Stigma* (New Brunswick, N.J.: Rutgers University Press, 1999).

35. See extended discussion in S. P. Hinshaw and D. Cicchetti, "Stigma and Mental Disorder: Conceptions of Illness, Public Attitudes, Personal Disclosure, and Social Policy," *Development and Psychopathology* 12 (2000): 555–98.

36. N. Sartorius, "Stigma: What Can Psychiatrists Do about It?" *Lancet* 352 (1998): 1058–59.

37. Hinshaw and Cicchetti, "Stigma and Mental Disorder," 563.

38. B. Geller and J. Luby, "Child and Adolescent Bipolar Disorder: A Review of the Past 10 Years," *Journal of the American Academy of Child and Adolescent Psychiatry* 36 (1997): 1169–76.

39. M. J. Gitlin, J. Swendsen, T. L. Heller, and C. Hammen, "Relapse and Impairment in Bipolar Disorder," *American Journal of Psychiatry* 152 (1995): 1635–40.

40. H. A. Sackeim, "The Anticonvulsant Hypothesis of the Mechanisms of Action of ECT: Current Status," *Journal of ECT* 15 (1999): 5–26.

41. H. A. Sackeim, D. P. Devanand, and M. S. Nobler, "Electroconvulsive Therapy," in F. E. Bloom and D. J. Kupfer, eds., *Psychopharmacology:*

The Fourth Generation of Progress (New York: Raven Press, 1995), 1123–41.

42. W. R. Beardslee, E. Wright, P. C. Rothberg, P. Salt, and E. Versage, "Response of Families to Two Preventive Intervention Strategies: Long-Term Differences in Behavior and Attitude Change," *Journal of the American Academy of Child and Adolescent Psychiatry* 35 (1996): 774–82.

43. Hinshaw and Cicchetti "Stigma and Mental Disorder," 555–98.

44. A clear statement of the need for such "translational" research that bridges basic science and clinical endeavors is found in Institute of Medicine, *Bridging Disciplines in the Brain, Behavioral, and Clinical Sciences* (Washington, D.C.: National Academy Press, 2000).

12. Resilience and Social Context

1. E. E. Werner and R. S. Smith, *Overcoming the Odds: High Risk Children from Birth to Adulthood* (Ithaca, N.Y.: Cornell University Press, 1992).

2. S. Luthar, D. Cicchetti, and B. Becker, "The Construct of Resilience: A Critical Evaluation and Guidelines for Future Work," *Child Development* 71 (2000): 543–62; W. R. Beardslee, "The Role of Self-Understanding in Resilient Individuals: The Development of a Perspective," *American Journal of Orthopsychiatry* 59 (1989): 266–78.

3. D. Cicchetti and N. Garmezy, eds., Special issue: "Milestones in the Development of Resilience," *Development and Psychopathology* 5 (1993): 497–774.

4. M. E. P. Seligman and M. Csikzentmihalyi, "Positive Psychology: An Introduction," *American Psychologist* 55 (2000): 5–14.

5. Werner and Smith, *Overcoming the Odds.*

6. Seligman and Csikentmihalyi, "Positive Psychology."

7. B. A. Esterling, L. L'Abate, E. J. Murray, and J. W. Pennebaker, "Empirical Foundations for Writing in Prevention and Psychotherapy: Mental and Physical Health Outcomes," *Clinical Psychology Review* 19 (1999): 79–96; J. W. Pennebaker, "Writing about Emotional Experiences as a Therapeutic Process," *Psychological Science* 8 (1997): 162–66.

8. A. Masten and N. Garmezy, "Risk, Vulnerability, and Protective Factors in Developmental Psychopathology," in B. B. Lahey and A. E. Kazdin, eds., *Advances in Clinical Child Psychology* (New York: Plenum Press, 1985), vol. 8, pp. 1–52.

9. S. P. Hinshaw and D. Cicchetti, "Stigma and Mental Disorder: Conceptions of Illness, Public Attitudes, Personal Disclosure, and Social Policy," *Development and Psychopathology* 12 (2000): 555–98; U.S. Department of Health and Human Services, *Mental Health: A Report of the Surgeon General* (Rockville, Md.: published by the author, 1999).

10. K. S. Kendler, J. M. Myers, and M. C. Neale, "A Multidimensional Twin Study of Mental Health in Women," *American Journal of Psychiatry* 157 (2000): 506–13.
11. M. Tsuang, "Genes, Environment, and Mental Health Wellness," *American Journal of Psychiatry* 157 (2000): 489–91.
12. Beardslee, "The Role of Self-Understanding in Resilient Individuals."
13. American Psychiatric Association, *Diagnostic and Statistical Manual of Mental Disorders*, 4th ed. (Washington, D.C.: American Psychiatric Press, 1994).
14. D. Fannon, X. Chitnis, V. Daku, and L. Tennakoon, "Features of Structural Brain Abnormalities Detected in First-Episode Psychosis," *American Journal of Psychiatry* 157 (2000): 1829–34; P. B. Jones and C. J. Tarrant, "Developmental Precursors and Biological Markers for Schizophrenia and Affective Disorders: Specificity and Public Health Implications," *European Archives of Psychiatry and Clinical Neuroscience* 250 (2000): 286–91.
15. K. Lin and A. Kleinman, "Psychopathology and the Clinical Course of Schizophrenia: A Cross-Cultural Perspective," *Schizophrenia Bulletin* 14 (1988): 555–67.
16. P. C. Whybrow, *A Mood Apart: Depression, Mania, and Other Afflictions of the Self* (New York: Basic Books, 1997).
17. R. Lewis, *The Other Great Depression* (New York: Public Affairs/Perseus Books, 2000).
18. R. Brown, *Social Psychology* (New York: Free Press, 1965); R. Kurzban and M. R. Leary, "Evolutionary Origins of Stigmatization: The Functions of Social Exclusion," *Psychological Bulletin* 127 (2001): 187–208.
19. Hinshaw and Cicchetti, "Stigma and Mental Disorder."
20. http://www.NYTimes.com/race.
21. P. W. Corrigan and D. L. Penn, "Lessons from Social Psychology on Discrediting Psychiatric Stigma," *American Psychologist* 54 (1999): 765–76.
22. J. W. Pennebaker and J. D. Seagal, "Forming a Story: The Health Benefits of Narrative," *Journal of Clinical Psychology* 55 (1999): 1243–54.
23. A partial list includes K. Cronkite, *On the Edge of Darkness: Conversations about Conquering Depression* (New York: Delta, 1994); K. R. Jamison, *An Unquiet Mind: A Memoir of Moods and Madness* (New York: Knopf, 1995); N. Lachenmeyer, *The Outsider* (New York: Random House, 2000); J. Neugeboren, *Imagining Robert: My Brother, Madness, and Survival* (New York: Henry Holt, 1998); J. Smith, *Where the Roots Reach for Water: A Personal and Natural History of Melancholia* (New York: North Point Press, 1999); A. Solomon, *The Noonday Demon: An Atlas of Depression* (New York: Scribner, 2001); W. Styron, *Darkness*

Visible: A Memoir of Madness (New York: Harper and Row, 1990). For a work of historical importance in the field, see B. Kaplan, ed., *The Inner World of Mental Illness* (New York: Harper and Row, 1964). For a focus on women, see R. Shannonhouse, ed., *Out of Her Mind: Women Writing on Madness* (New York: Modern Library, 2000).

24. E.g., the major motion picture, *A Beautiful Mind*, released just before the time of the final writing of this work, stars Russell Crowe and exemplifies the current climate of wider public exposure to – and, potentially, acceptance of – severe mental disorder. This film, based on the biography of John Nash by Sylvia Nasar, has greatly simplified Nash's complex life yet still manages to portray a moving and realistic account of psychotic behavior. See A. O. Scott, "Math, Madness, and Back: A Journey," *New York Times*, December 21, 2001, pp. E1, E37.

25. W. R. Beardslee, E. Wright, P. C. Rothberg, P. Salt, and E. Versage, "Response of Families to Two Preventive Intervention Strategies: Long-Term Differences in Behavior and Attitude Change," *Journal of the American Academy of Child and Adolescent Psychiatry* 35 (1996): 774–82.

13. A Son's Perspective

1. S. H. Barondes, *Mood Genes: Hunting for the Origins of Mania and Depression* (New York: Freeman, 1998). On the other hand, if a child's parents both have the disorder, the risk to the offspring rises rather dramatically.

2. K. R. Jamison, "Stigma of Manic-Depression: A Psychologist's Experience," *Lancet* 352 (1998): 1053.

3. O. F. Wahl, *Telling Is Risky Business: Mental Health Consumers Confront Stigma* (New Brunswick, N.J.: Rutgers University Press, 1999). For perspective on the stigmatization received by medical students and residents in their training careers and the barriers to openness in the medical and health professions in general, see L. J. Dickstein and L. D. Heinz, "The Stigma of Mental Illness for Medical Students and Residents," in P. J. Fink and A. Tasman, eds., *Stigma and Mental Illness* (Washington, D.C.: American Psychiatric Press, 1992), 153–65.

4. K. R. Jamison, *An Unquiet Mind: A Memoir of Moods and Madness* (New York: Knopf, 1995).

Index

Index

Index

psychotic experiences/episodes, *see* psychosis
punishment, 24–5, 28–30, 32, 42, 43, 54, 61, 70, 121, 142–4, 186

Quaker, 14, 17, 24, 40, 43, 44, 193

racism, 194–5
religion: religious background, 14; religious faith, 36, 188; religious themes, 36; religious thoughts, 54; religious training, 24, 31, 39
resilience, 6, 185–91
Robinson, Jackie, 31, 160
Rose Bowl, 39
Russell, Bertrand, 43, 136, 160

schizoaffective disorder, 20, 124
schizophrenia, 11, 20, 55, 58, 81, 85, 97, 104, 111, 123–4, 131, 150n, 191, 192; differentiation from bipolar disorder, 90–4; negative symptoms in, 95; schizophrenic psychosis, 38
Schou, Mogens, 96, 126–7, 133–5
self-concept, *see* self-image
self-destruction, *see* suicide
self-image, 6, 36, 143, 146, 169, 174, 180
separation anxiety, 72
silence, 8, 9, 63, 65, 71, 80, 103, 138, 143, 146, 188, 196, 198–200, 202, 207, 210
sleep: fear of not falling asleep, 71–3, 111–14; sleep-wake cycles, 89, 171

sleeplessness, 11, 50, 106, 113, 115, 116, 160
social support, 192
sports: baseball, 31, 62, 66–8, 72; football, 31, 48, 62, 77, 78; shotput, 31
Stanford University, 38, 39, 40, 151, 154
stigma, 4, 5, 8, 22, 98, 176, 177, 181, 183, 190, 195, 197, 208
stigmatization, *see* stigma
substance abuse, 83, 89, 117, 121, 179, 207
suicide, 37, 88, 101, 134, 174; suicide risk, 82
support groups, 134–5, 175, 181
Surgeon General, 3, 65

tardive dyskinesia, 98, 101
Thorazine, 52, 58
thought disorder, 20, 94, 95, 100

University of California, Berkeley, 20, 38, 139, 140, 154, 209
University of California, Los Angeles (UCLA), 117, 120, 127, 133, 139, 140, 154, 187n; Affective Disorders Clinic, 126–8, 131, 135, 152–3; Neuropsychiatric Institute, 126, 131

valedictorian, 39, 80
vomiting, 113–14, 115–16

White House Conference on Mental Health, 3
World War II, 41, 43, 193

227